CASTAWAYS

The Penikese Island Experiment

George Cadwalader

CHELSEA GREEN PUBLISHING COMPANY
White River Junction, Vermont

Printed on recycled paper.

First Chelsea Green Classics edition printing February, 2007.

Chelsea Green Classics edition
ISBN 978-1-933392-20-2

**The Library of Congress has catalogued the previous
edition as follows:**
Cadwalader, George, 1939-
    Castaways : the Penikese Island experiment.
  1. Reformatories—Massachusetts—Case studies.
2. Rehabilitation of juvenile delinquents—Massachusetts—
Case studies. I. Title.
HV9105.M4C32 1988 .   365'.974494   87-17891
ISBN 0-930031-12-1 (alk. paper)

Chelsea Green Publishing Company
PO Box 428
White River Junction, Vermont 05001
802-295-6300
www.chelseagreen.com

for
Yara and Franny

FOREWORD

THIRTY YEARS AGO I was working with so-called "delinquent" youths in one of the "reform schools" the author of this extraordinary book mentions early on — the Lancaster Industrial School (for girls). In fact, the place wasn't as bad as some of its critics would allege during the turbulent 1960s. It had been founded as yet another effort to help troubled youth find a new life for themselves, not on an island, as is the case with the project George Cadwalader describes, but in the magically bucolic countryside of an old New England town well to the west of Boston. I will never forget what one of the youths "sent" there (by court order) said to me one day about the countryside she largely, alas, ignored: "It's pretty nice out here, if you feel like enjoying the scenery."

She was letting a young child psychiatrist know what poets have told all of us over the generations, that, as the saying goes, beauty is in the eye of the beholder. She was, really, speaking of an irony — the pastoral loveliness of rolling New England farm country as against the grim, melancholy landscape of her own mind. She was a tough, foul-mouthed, truculent young lady who sneered at anyone and everyone, told me off constantly as I tried to have conversations with her, and one day sobbed uncontrollably as, finally, she let me know the awful particulars of her much-abused childhood.

I thought of her as I read this truly remarkable and valuable book — the finest account of firsthand work with troubled and "anti-social" youth since August Aichhorn's *Wayward Youth*. The author is wonderfully candid and self-critical, utterly uninterested in presenting himself to the reader as God's magnificent gift to hurt, difficult children, and by extension, to all humanity. If anything, he is his own tough, skeptical critic, all too aware of the disappointments and defeats he and his colleagues have experienced, and of the demonic side of human nature as it tenaciously exerts itself on certain young people. He offers us no unqualified answers, only the occasional redemptive possibilities which are to be found, so often unpredictably, in one or another person. He offers us, really, himself — a thoughtful and decent person who has known his fair share of tragedy, seen the violence people can inflict on one another (in the wars we seem unable to stop waging on this planet) and who has tried, in this "experiment," as he so modestly puts it, to do his best for others, however turbulent and unpromising their lives.

I want to sing the praises of this book. The tenth chapter, with its Faulknerian entry into a tortured mind driven to torture, is a masterpiece of psychological analysis. A quiet, at times brooding lyricism is at work in the pages that follow — of a kind not at all inappropriate to the subject matter: the thwarted lives of young people who, surely, deserve the kind of attentive concern the author has given them, the talent of deed and word he has summoned here on their behalf.

Cadwalader worries about his failures, but his successes are substantial. Lord knows, the rest of us ought bow our heads gratefully toward his; thank him for his everyday presentation to needy others of time and thought and energy; salute him gratefully for the additional gift of this splendid and lucid book, which radiates the moral energy of commitment and is written so compellingly and vividly. Many will be lost to George Cadwalader as he and his friends continue their efforts on Penikese Island; but some will, indeed, be touched, and ultimately born to new lives by virtue of such efforts — what in an earlier time without embarrassment would have been called the Lord's work, and what some of us today will most definitely want to describe in a similar vein.

ROBERT COLES

PREFACE

T HIS IS THE STORY of an experiment that would appear to have failed. It tells of the effort, begun in the summer of 1973 by a group of friends and me, to start a school for delinquent teenage boys on remote Penikese Island in Buzzards Bay off the Massachusetts coast. In the years that followed its establishment the Penikese Island School drew the kind of publicity that quixotic pursuits of this kind generally attract, particularly if they occupy picturesque locations. The newspaper and television coverage we received contained all the predictable superlatives. Our "no-nonsense" curriculum was "unique." Our staff was "caring," and our students were quoted talking earnestly of "turning themselves around." All of this was true. And yet when in 1980 we followed up on the first 106 boys who had come to Penikese, we discovered what by then we had already begun to suspect. In fact only sixteen had "turned themselves around." The other ninety had gone on to lives destructive in varying degrees to themselves and others.

When we began the school we had seen ourselves as part of a pioneering new partnership between the public and private sectors in which Massachusetts' archaic reform schools would be replaced by a whole range of private schools and programs, all bringing different approaches to the common goal of helping kids in trouble. Jerome Miller, the man credited with bringing about this reform, had just left the state on a wave of national publicity to carry his crusade to Illinois. In Massachusetts his work would be carried forward by the young idealists who had marched with him in his demonstrations against the reform schools and who had routed the reactionary elements from the state Department of Youth Services, which they now controlled. Punishment was out. Rehabilitation was in. No longer would young people be forced to suffer for the crimes of an unjust society.

At Penikese we were from the start a little uneasy about some of the assumptions and most of the rhetoric of this new movement, but in general we shared its goals. So it was all the more disappointing when we realized that we had instead bought into a system that, despite many good people within it, still managed, through its own muddleheadedness, only to produce in the minds of those it sought to help the same feelings of powerless confusion that more than anything else had led them into delinquency in the first place.

The odd thing, in view of these many miscalculations, is that the four of us who started Penikese were all too old to be entirely naive. David Masch had for ten years been working as a field biologist for the Woods Hole Oceanographic Institution. My ten-year career as a Marine had been ended by a mine explosion in Viet Nam. Herman Bosch was a merchant-marine officer with a doctorate in oceanography, and Carl "Chip" Jackson was an Annapolis graduate who had left the Navy to study art. We were all over thirty, which made us old men by the youthful standards of the business we were getting into.

None of us had been drawn to Penikese entirely by untempered idealism. Although the motivations for our involvement differed, one common attraction the school offered was the chance to turn the kind of lifestyle we enjoyed into a vocation. We were all sufficiently in the thrall of that ridiculous Puritan legacy which differentiates between work and fun to find the idea of days spent fishing and sailing somehow less frivolous if the end result was to help kids. We were also the products of John F. Kennedy's Camelot. We wanted to do some good.

In one respect, however, we were every bit as innocent as even the most wide-eyed of the reformers who had flocked to Jerome Miller's banner. We shared without question the assumption that bad kids were simply the products of bad environments. We believed changing the environment could change the kid, and we thought that by combining the experiences of our diverse backgrounds we could devise the kind of Huck Finn world that would bring out the good hidden in even the most cynical delinquent.

We are no longer so sure of ourselves. Some of the boys who have come to Penikese have in fact been basically intact kids driven into delinquency by social pressures. But these kids are a minority, a minority, oddly, that more often than not conforms most closely to the surly "punk-kid" image associated with the delinquent. Most of our students, by contrast, don't on the face of it look or act much different from any random sampling of "straight" teenagers of the same ages. They do not conform to any obvious generalizations about intelligence, background or personality; a little rougher around the edges perhaps, but on the whole these kids look just like the kid down the street. Visitors to Penikese usually arrive expecting to step into a Blackboard Jungle and leave remarking, "What a nice bunch of boys!"

This impression, sadly, does not square with the facts. Those first 106 boys we followed up were collectively charged between 1973 and 1980 with 309 violent and 3,082 nonviolent crimes. Despite their Oliver Twist charm, our kids have shown us a darker side. They appear incapable of love, driven by unfocused anger, and prone to impulsive behavior without regard to consequences. This last characteristic, the logical end-product of Madison Avenue's exhortations to instant gratification, can, when coupled with the first two, produce the terrifying kind of emotionless brutality that led one of our kids to break the legs of all our chickens.

We have found, not surprisingly, that the general public doesn't want to hear about those chickens. The same people who turn out to watch scenes of carnage produced by Hollywood are made sick at the thought of a boy systematically maiming helpless birds. They would prefer to read the kind of upbeat accounts of delinquent rehabilitation that appear from time to time in the media, telling of charismatic programs for troubled children which claim 75-percent success rates for their graduates. I wish these programs well, but I wonder if they are working with the same kids we are. Because when I look objectively at the trail of destruction left by our own graduates, I cannot avoid the conclusion that the world would have been a better place if most of the kids I grew to like at Penikese had never been born. I think of Rick, who hates women so much that he openly fantasizes of "killing broads an' buryin' 'em in my cellar," and I recall the many other walking time bombs like him whom we have watched leave the island knowing that they cannot be stopped until they have exploded at horrible cost in human suffering. I get a letter from Andy—"Hey George, I got good news and I got bad news! Good news is I'm gonna be a father. Bad news is I'm in Walpole, 10 to 20"—and I wonder how many other of our alumni have already fathered probably doomed children of their own.

Such thoughts as these lead me inevitably to consideration of the nightmarish questions our society must confront if it ever seeks seriously to eliminate its violent fringe. How many chances does an individual deserve before we are justified in giving up on him? What do we do with those we have given up on? Beyond these issues lie even greater moral quagmires for those who have renounced rehabilitation as an achievable strategy. If not rehabilitation, what? Forced sterilization? Giant prisons? The death penalty? Selective breeding? There are scary times when I find myself less repelled in principle by such draconian solutions than I am deterred from their serious consideration by the certainty that whatever public agencies were created for their implementation would inevitably be incompetent. In any event Penikese has not led me to any revelations on these issues, but working there has made them harder to ignore.

This, then, is not only the story of a school but also of the fall from innocence of those who started it. Penikese still continues. Despite our disillusionment we have not been able to give it up. In my case I can no longer say whether my motivation for going on is simply the inability to admit that the past fourteen years have gone for nothing or whether, despite all evidence to the contrary, I continue to hang on to the hope that what we set out to do is still not impossible and that what we have done has not been wasted. David Masch is more sanguine than I, less discouraged by gloomy statistics and more willing to trust his instincts, which tell him that even with our most damaged kids Penikese has done some good, however hard that is to define. He is probably right. How do you measure success in this business? If Penikese has managed to defuse a potential murderer to the point that he limits his crimes to car theft, is that not success?

Whatever the verdict on that question, I know that no inner-city kid who has taken the long boat ride to Penikese and there listened to the mysterious night calls of the petrels and watched the moon rising over Buzzards Bay is likely ever to forget those experiences. Some fated for later misery may look back on the island as a place where they were briefly happy, and that alone may be all we can hope to offer them.

Before you read any further, I must warn you that this book is filled with the most disgusting kind of profanity. I first tried substituting X!!#*! for offending words, but this comic-book device didn't work. Dialogue consisting almost entirely of symbols makes for dull reading. It also paints a very sterile picture of the kids this story is all about. So I have written down what they say the way they say it.

My one concession to propriety has been to juggle names, chronologies and events sufficiently to protect the identities of our students. All the adults in the book are in theory at least responsible for their own behavior, so I have left them with their real names. The story itself is a true one, except in Chapter 10 where I try to recreate what was going through the head of the boy who maimed our chickens. We never found out who this boy was so my account must be fictional. The attitudes it describes are real.

If I were to thank all the people responsible for making this book possible, this prologue would be longer than the story which follows it. Without the school there would have been no book, and I hope the many unmentioned friends who have made Penikese what it is will accept my thanks for their efforts and my apologies for not including their names here.

Two people do need to be singled out. One is my friend Ian Baldwin, whose idea this book was and whose exacting standards as its editor have nearly driven me nuts. The other is Franny Shepherd, who typed this story many times and whose countless acts of kindness to all of us at Penikese remind me in the face of often conflicting evidence that decency and generosity of spirit are achievable goals.

"Society has made them its enemies.
Therefore weak though they be they
will wage such war as they can."

Dr. Frank Parker writing in 1905 of
the lepers who were then quarantined
for life on Penikese Island.

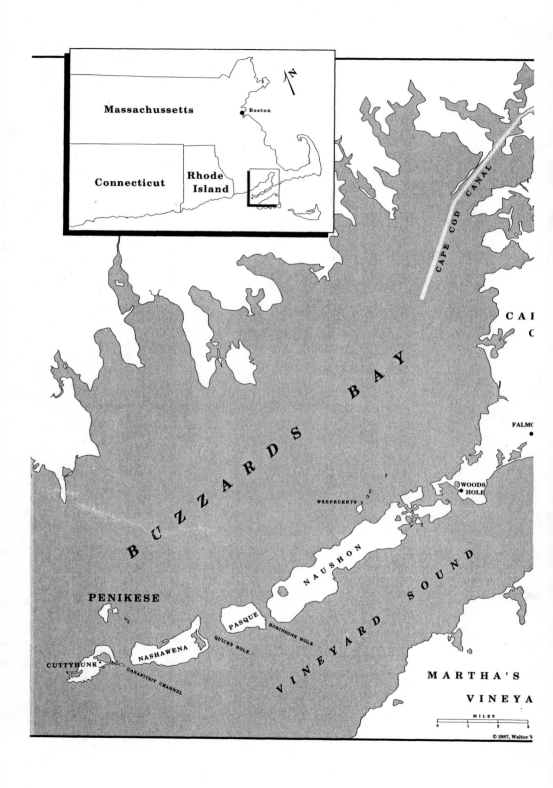

Massachussetts

Boston

Connecticut

Rhode
Island

CAPE COD CANAL

CAI
C

B U Z Z A R D S   B A Y

WEEPECKETS

FALMO

WOODS
HOLE

PENIKESE

NAUSHON

PASQUE

ROBINSONS HOLE

QUICK'S HOLE

NASHAWENA

V I N E Y A R D   S O U N D

CUTTYHUNK

CANAPITSIT CHANNEL

MARTHA'S

VINEYA

MILES

0   1   2   3

© 1987, Walter V

1

T HE NOVEMBER NIGHT had fallen early, and the hard west wind was kicking up a nasty swell across the mile of open water between Penikese Island and neighboring Cuttyhunk. We had spent that late-fall day in 1973 raising the roof of the building that was to become home to the more than two hundred delinquent teenage boys who were to live for varying periods of time on Penikese during the next fourteen years.

Five of our first six students had worked hard and well, caught up as we were in the race against winter and the growing excitement of watching the house take shape. "Christ," muttered tough little Jack through a mouthful of nails, "this ain't like no fuckin' school. This is work!"

His four colleagues, all longtime street veterans, profanely agreed. Stan, the sixth boy, said nothing. Lost as usual in his mood of sullen rebellion, he had contrived all day to slink away whenever we needed him most. Our own efforts to shame him into greater effort, along with the unflattering comments of his colleagues, added self-pity to his other woes, and by the time we set out for our temporary living quarters aboard an old coastal freighter moored in Cuttyhunk Harbor, Stan was in a foul frame of mind.

I picked him to drive the boat. "Aw, come on, man, I been bustin' my ass all day," he whined, with notable disregard for fact. Nonetheless he took the wheel, and we cast off into the wind and night. It was a rough trip. *Nereis*, the donated fifty-year-old fishing boat in which we commuted to and from Penikese, rolled horribly in the steep beam sea. Stan looked apprehensively at me, started to say something and thought better of it. The startled faces of the other kids popped up from the cabin to find Stan hanging grimly onto the wheel, his features an eerie green in the reflected glare of the starboard running light. Sheets of spray cascaded over the boat. "Stan, man, you're gonna get us all killed," shouted Bill as he ducked back below.

The ghost of a grin crossed Stan's face. He plainly had a good feel for the boat. By the time we were halfway across he was meeting each oncoming sea, spinning the boat neatly across the top of it and slipping her smoothly into the trough beyond. His fears forgotten, he started having fun. We rounded the breakwater into the comparative calm of Cuttyhunk Harbor and strained to make out the bulk of the old freighter in the pitch darkness. Landing alongside our floating dormitory was always a bit of a trick in any kind of a wind, and by now it was really howling. I started to take the wheel, but seeing the look of furious concentration on Stan's face changed my mind.

The old hulk loomed up in front of us. For a moment it looked as if we would hit her; Stan spun the wheel, backed down hard and *Nereis* slid in to a perfect landing. He looked at me with a huge boyish grin. The other kids crowded around him, and the six of them jumped across to the old freighter, laughing and shouting, the day's fights and arguments temporarily forgotten.

"Jeesus, did you see them fuckin' waves?"

"Hey! Can Stan drive that boat or what?"

"Shit! That's the only thing he done all day was drive the boat."

"What are ya talking about? I worked my fuckin' balls off!"

"What balls?"

Their voices faded down the companionway, leaving behind only the wailing of the wind in the ancient cargo boom above my head. I doubled up on *Nereis'* lines and groped my way across the deck to check on *Sagitta*, the other vessel in our venerable fleet. By the lights from the houses on Cuttyhunk I could see the tops blowing off the whitecaps in the harbor, and I was glad we hadn't waited any longer to come across.

We called our floating home the Frenchman in preference to her real name, which nobody could pronounce. Many years before she had carried freight to remote settlements along the Labrador coast. In her old age she had limped south to founder on a sand bar in Cape Cod Bay, where she lay until salvaged by my friend, Dan Clark, a marine contractor who had fitted her out with crude bunks and a giant wood-burning cook stove for use as a crew boat. We had borrowed her to live on while we built the house on Penikese.

Now she was rolling ponderously before the vicious gusts of wind that slammed across the harbor. A few big drops of rain began battering against the wheelhouse windows, but I was enjoying this moment of unexpected solitude and was in no hurry to go below. *Sagitta* was pounding hard against her fenders. Chip Jackson had brought her across an hour previously to start dinner, and from the amount of water in her he must have had a hell of a trip. Chip had been my hospital roommate when I was a Viet Nam casualty. He had, as he put it, "fallen for his country" playing pickup basketball at Submarine School in New London. Four years later he had resigned his commission to study art, and now he was interrupting his new career to help me and two other friends start the school on Penikese. The four of us were then working alternating shifts of three days each, and that night Chip and I had the duty.

I streamed *Sagitta* off on a long line behind the Frenchman and climbed down the companionway to the already familiar scene below. The six kids milled noisily in and out of the dim circles of light cast by the kerosene lanterns that swayed from the overhead. Ahead of me the cavernous hold stretched away into the darkness, and to my left, beneath the bright halo from our single gas lamp, stood Chip, serenely presiding over two huge caldrons atop the glowing stove. Jack appeared out of the darkness at his side. He looked skeptically into the pot.

"Hey, Chip, what're we havin'?"

"Spaghetti. What's it look like?"

"Looks like shit, man! What're ya gonna put on it?"

"I made a sauce of those quahogs we raked up. Damn good, if I do say so!"

"Yeah? Them quahogs is fish, ain't they?"

"Shellfish, yes."

"Well then, I ain't eatin' none! Fish sucks!"

Over at the big oak table that ran the length of the hold Duane was drawing a picture. A big late-fall fly came alive in the rising heat and began buzzing clumsily around his head. Duane reached up with the unconscious grace of the natural athlete and grabbed it out of the air. He slammed it down on the table and examined the corpse curiously.

"Hey Bill! Come 'ere! This fucker ain't got no blood in 'im. Got some kinda white shit instead."

Bill joined him at the table, followed by Danny. Their heads bent seriously over the late fly.

"That's pus," announced Nick, who knew everything.

"Nah! looks like the stuff they put in doughnuts. Ya know, the cream ones?"

"Wonder what he tastes like? Ya ever eat a fly, Danny? Kid I knew up at Rozie, he'd eat flies an' all kindsa shit. He was hard, man!"

Chip looked up. He could see it coming, and so could I.

Poor Danny, the perennial sucker, bit. "Sure I eats flies. What'll ya give me if I eats one?"

"That butt you was tryin' to bum from me on the boat. I'll give you that butt."

Danny started backpeddling. "Gotta be a Marlboro."

"Only got Kents. Ya got Marlboros, Nick?"

"Yeah, I got 'em." Nick shoved a cigarette over to Danny. "Here! Now come on! Eat that motha!"

Danny was desperate. "Nah, I only eat 'em when they're alive. Don't eat 'em squished. No way!"

Chip to the rescue. "Time to eat! Come on, you turkeys! Get rid of that damn fly and set the table."

Danny saw his escape and rushed over to grab the plates. The others followed, but I knew Danny only had a reprieve. From then on it was going to be open season on live flies.

The kids lined up at the stove. Chip ladled out huge piles of spaghetti onto each plate until he got to Jack.

"Don't want none, man. I told you already. Fish fuckin' sucks! I'm gonna make me a peanut-butter sandwich."

"No you're not, goddamnit! You know the rules. You eat what we got or you don't eat at all. You eat up all the bread now, and we won't have any for breakfast."

Jack's Irish temper flared. "Fuck, man! You ain't gonna stop me. Where's that fuckin' bread?"

Chip stood impassively in front of him. The other kids fell silent. Jack backed off. "OK, man. Gimme some o' that spaghetti, but don't put none o' that other shit on top of it. Put it over to the side, like, so's I can pick them fuckin' woe-whos out."

"Quahogs!"

"Whatever!"

Jack couldn't stay angry long. He went back to the table and was soon chattering away with the rest of them. I sat at the end, looking down the row of shadowy faces on either side of the table. The kids all wore long mops of hair which required frequent tosses of the head to flip it back out of their plates. One would lead off with this comical twisting jerk, and the rest would unconsciously follow, like coughers at a concert. Usually they also wore their hard street faces, but that night in the soft light of the lanterns they looked like the boys they so rarely dared to be.

Jack was all the way down at the end. Hunger had triumphed over prejudice and he was munching away on the quahogs. He looked up with his mouth full. "Hey, Chip. You been shittin' me. This stuff's meat!"

"Nope. It's shellfish."

"Nah, it's meat. Gotta be. This is good. Fish sucks."

So passed our first fall on Penikese. As the days got colder we grew accustomed to finding ice in the Frenchman's sink each morning. "Colder than a witch's prick!" announced Duane, who never got his metaphors quite right. It was dark when we left Cuttyhunk in the morning and dark when we got back at night. More and more often we woke up to find it blowing too hard to risk the trip across, and on such days we learned that inactivity brought out the worst in our charges. Violence was never very far from the surface in their lives, and boredom made short fuses shorter. Most of the time, however, we were able to keep their hands and minds productively occupied, which for the most of them was a new experience. Even Bill, our most ardent clock watcher, occasionally got so caught up in the effort to get the house closed in that he would work right through coffee break, to his later dismay when he realized what he'd done. "Hey!" would come his outraged shriek from the roof. "It's already past fuckin' lunch time, an' we ain't even stopped for fuckin' coffee yet! You guys is the fuckin' worst, man! Even fuckin' *Hitler* gives coffee breaks!"

Harder weather also made trips to Woods Hole more uncertain, and the staff's shifts on the island were often prolonged. I remember one time in particular when Herman Bosch and I found ourselves marooned with the kids for three additional days. Herman snored like a steam whistle, which meant that if I didn't get to sleep before he did I might not sleep at all. I usually snuck off to our staff quarters in the pilot house in time to get a head start on him, but on the night that sticks in my memory I got involved in a chess game with Danny, and by the time I finally got up to bed, Herman was already making the rafters ring. It was too cold to move outside, so I lay there in that state of half-sleep which sets your mind off in strange directions, and I recall thinking of Private Padgett and Fred Mangelsdorf and Frank Carey, and the odd way in which apparently unrelated people and events seem, in retrospect, to fit together with a coherence that appears almost preordained.

2

PADGETT COULD NOT have known when he fell to a sniper's bullet in a Viet Nam rice paddy that he, or more properly, his memory, would be instrumental in bringing together six boys very much like him on a rusty freighter in Cuttyhunk Harbor. I had first met him two years before he died, when I was a gung-ho new company commander of a reconnaissance company at Camp Lejeune and he was my newest recruit. In those days "Recon," despite its pretensions to elitism, actually served as a dumping ground for rejects from the rest of the division. We had learned to expect the worst whenever we got a new draft from the line companies, but even so Padgett came as a shock. "Christ," moaned my first sergeant as he surveyed a service record that bulged with testimony to Padgett's career in crime, "they're sending us Al Capone!"

With that introduction I had expected to meet someone quite different from the frail, scared boy who sullenly presented himself for duty. As it was I took malicious pleasure in assigning Padgett to the platoon leader who had just beaten me in a foot race. Shortly thereafter the company went off to the field to practice land navigation, and to our amazement, our new recruit demonstrated an instinctive sense of direction which made him nearly infallible at finding his way across country. He was as unaware of this talent as we were, and he fairly burst with pride when he proved the best among us with the compass.

From that day forward Padgett had become a different person. In contrast to his former sullen self, he developed into something of an extrovert, with a wonderfully dry sense of humor. More surprising yet, he became a physical-fitness nut, and in due course there were two in that platoon who could outrun me. Padgett and I became friends in the kind of unspoken way that friendships develop between officers and enlisted men, and later, at a time when Marines I knew were dying at a rate that left me incapable of much more than dumb shock, I recall feeling more than that when I learned Padgett had been killed.

During the ten years that I spent in the Marine Corps, I met many other kids who, like Padgett, had enlisted to avoid "time." Some of them belonged in jail, but most had found in the Marines the same structure, excitement and sense of belonging that gang life had provided on the street. I liked those ex-delinquents a lot. They were tough, high spirited, loyal, funny and fair; the kind of kids that later at Penikese we labeled somewhat nostalgically as "old-fashioned delinquents."

A mine explosion in another Viet Nam rice paddy had ended my own career in the Marine Corps, and I had found myself at age thirty a retired major with a wife and child and very little idea about what to do next. As early as I could remember, my father had steered me towards doing "something worthwhile." The Marine Corps met that test. I had joined up planning just to "do my time" and to my own surprise ended up a "lifer." One event that contributed to this conversion occurred when, as a still-green lieutenant attached to the Sixth Fleet in the Mediterranean, I took leave to go see the palace in Austria where Hayden had been court composer. I got lost and stumbled instead on a torn-up section of the Iron Curtain where a Hungarian family had died trying to escape to freedom. That sight had convinced me that we were not just playing games. The bad guys, in those days at least, really were bad.

During the months after Viet Nam that I spent in the hospital pondering my future, I considered going to medical school. That idea died when I discovered that my liberal-arts education condemned me to four more years as an undergraduate before I could even apply. So I took a job at the Woods Hole Oceanographic Institution, hoping to find there work that was both fun and worthwhile.

The Oceanographic was a wonderful place, but my ignorance of math and science limited my role there to the kind of administrative tasks I neither enjoyed nor was very good at. Fortunately there was a policy that administrators should occasionally go along on research cruises to learn what the business of the Oceanographic was all about. Seeing this as a way to escape from my desk, I had signed up for a biology cruise on the research vessel *Gosnold*, with Dr. Frank Carey. Biologists are the most irreverent of oceanographers and are not charitably disposed toward administrators. The prospect of my company met with limited enthusiasm by the scientific party.

Frank's work involved the study of certain large fishes that are able to regulate their body temperatures independent of water temperature. For this cruise he had signed on his brother, Brian, who later went on to prominence in the restaurant business, but who at the time was engaged in baiting the Establishment — of which he took me to be a representative. David Masch, also a man of strong opinions, was in charge of catching the fish for Frank to study, while Peter Laue, a microbiologist turned carpenter, came along to test a water sampler he had built and proved an effective ally to Brian's attacks on the military-industrial complex (which was funding the cruise). Also along was a mysterious fellow from another lab who resembled Count Dracula and who would issue forth whenever a fish was caught to draw off its blood and then return to his cabin where, it was suspected, he drank the contents of his syringe.

Frank caught his fish with a three-mile array of baited hooks that we set at night and retrieved the following morning. Time not so engaged was largely spent in the galley, where Brian would pour vitriol on the same evil capitalists that now fatten at his restaurants. David and Peter would heap scorn on the military, and I would shock them all with rightist, red-neck sentiments that made the assembled multitude foam with rage. None of us had any way of foreseeing that these same arguments, with many of the same cast, would continue later on Penikese.

When we got back to Woods Hole and I returned to my desk, I became even more unhappy, since Frank's cruise had shown me that others at the Oceanographic were engaged in the kinds of things I would have infinitely preferred doing myself. As it was I went from one clerical task to another until at length I found myself work-

ing for Fred Mangelsdorf, the Oceanographic's assistant director
(I was assistant to the director) who was overseeing construction
of the Institution's new laboratory. Fred had an extraordinarily
well-organized mind and was interested in a great variety of sub-
jects, for each one of which he maintained a file of relevant news
clippings and the like. One of these files was labeled Crime and
Corrections.

Fred and I would frequently junket off to New York to confer
with the designers of the new lab. At these meetings he would
closet himself with the senior partners to discuss matters of policy
while I would meet with the lesser functionaries to talk about the
placement of doors. We would then all repair to a sumptuous lunch,
the cost of which must have added significantly to the price of the
building. Then Fred and I would fly back to Boston. During one
of these trips I mentioned to him my disenchantment with my
job and told him I was thinking of writing to Outward Bound to
see if that organization had anything I was better suited for.

Fred's computerlike brain had begun to whir, the Crime and Corrections file was mentally summoned up, and he began reciting from
a recent news article he had read reporting on Massachusetts' effort to replace its reform schools with private programs that, it was
hoped, would prove more effective at rehabilitating kids in trouble. Why not, he asked, start my own Outward Bound-type program for delinquents.

We were flying at the time over the Elizabeth Islands, which
stretch westward from Woods Hole to Cuttyhunk. I looked out the
window over this last stretch of really wild coastline left in Massachusetts and thought to myself what a perfect place these islands
would be for the kind of project Fred was suggesting. Why not do
it? Starting a school that would make hurting children whole again
was one way for a liberal-arts major to become the doctor I had
wanted to be.

By the time Fred and I landed in Boston, I was filled with excitement about his idea. I thought of Padgett, and I dreamed of
a school on one of the Elizabeth Islands that would do for other
boys what the Marine Corps had done for him. During the drive
back to Woods Hole we stopped for a dinner which, following that

lunch in New York, put me in a mellow mood indeed. As Fred's face swam mistily before me, I conjured up a future spent at sailing, at farming, at boat building, at all the things I loved to do, now given purpose by the boys who would share in these pursuits and in the process change their lives for the better.

The following morning I woke up with a horrible hangover and the awful realization that I couldn't remember what the architects and I had decided to do about those damn doors. As to my dreams of an island school, these came close to foundering on the sobering memory of another Marine, this one named Johnson.

Private Johnson had joined my company shortly after Padgett and had brought with him a record that was only slightly better. Unlike Padgett, he was a big, strong boy who looked like he belonged on a recruiting poster. From occasional unannounced visits to the barracks, I got the impression that he was a bit of a loudmouth, but to the NCOs and me he was always at pains to appear the model Marine. I found it hard to square his past record with his present performance and soon began to flatter myself with the thought that once again we had salvaged another misfit from Division.

Soon after Johnson's arrival things began disappearing from his squad bay. Johnson, whose size and mouth had won him a following, began hinting that Padgett was the culprit. Padgett, of course, was in misery until one of the squad leaders caught Johnson red-handed and took justice into his own hands behind the barracks.

All this I did not learn until later. So when Johnson came back two days late from liberty with a tale about having to stay home with his sick mother, I was inclined to believe him. My NCOs by then recognized him for what he was, but I was still caught up in the heady thought that even though others had failed I could still bring out the good in Johnson. At Office Hours he stood before my desk, the picture of contriteness, as he pleaded for one more chance. "You won't regret it, Lieutenant. Honest you won't!"

To the first sergeant's disgust, I let Johnson off with a slap on the wrist. A week later he cleaned out the barracks, stole a car and deserted. "I told you, Lieutenant," said the first sergeant. "That son of a bitch was born bad, and ain't you or anyone else gonna change him."

We argued the point. Nobody, I maintained, was "born bad." Johnson had shown us he had potential, and it had been our failure that we hadn't been able to bring it out in him. "Horseshit!" roared the Top. "Prob'ly they teach you that crap in college, but I'll tell you, sir, in the thirty years I've been in this lash-up, I've seen some, if they weren't born fucked up, then somebody sure as hell got to 'em pretty quick to make 'em that way!"

With the cockiness of youth I was unimpressed by the evidence of someone else's thirty years. Still, Johnson's inexplicable behavior hit me pretty hard. I was the one who had trusted him. I had given him a second chance, and he had shit on my head. I took it very personally.

There was another mystery as well. I had thought people became criminals because they were failures at everything else. Yet there was Johnson, apparently with all the equipment to be successful, electing to steal from his friends. It was all very puzzling for the short time I'd spent worrying about it. Johnson ended up in the brig, and I forgot all about him until I woke up that morning in Woods Hole.

Now, hung over and filled with guilt at having nothing to show from my New York junket, I reconsidered Fred's suggestion in a more sober frame of mind. But my spirits rose as my hangover receded, and the doubts raised by the spectre of Johnson gave way to renewed enthusiasm. The question became, How to begin?

As a result of my neglect of duty in the days that followed, men of science are still confounded by the labyrinth of randomly placed doors I created in the Oceanographic's new laboratory. Even more than usual, my mind at the time was on other things. Whom could I persuade to join me in this venture? How could I get access to one of the Elizabeth Islands? Would the State be receptive? And finally, what exactly would this school of mine do to work Padgett-like transformations in the lives of its students?

I thought back on the turning points in my own life and realized that most of these had been heralded by some dramatic event, usually a traumatic one. New schools, new neighborhoods, death in the family; such things as those had, it seemed, always led me to a change of course. In retrospect the most relevant of these experiences to what I was now trying to do began when I enrolled in the Marine Corps Officers Candidate School at Quantico, Virginia in the summer of 1960.

I had been one of a group of cocky college students who had climbed off the train at Quantico to be met by a giant drill instructor who surveyed us with disgust as he formed us up into awkward ranks. "OK, you college pukes, listen up!" he roared. "You're in the Marine Corps now, but you *ain't Marines*! You got that? What you is is *candidates* to be Marines, an' from the looks o' you scumbags, ain't none o' you gonna make it! Fuckin' college boys! *Shee-ut*! Fuckin' *brains*! What this outfit needs is *balls*, an' here they go an' send me you bunch o' candy-ass *brains*!"

The man next to me laughed nervously. Our DI swung around. For a long moment he let the tension build in the awful silence which followed. Then he moved slowly to within inches of my unfortunate neighbor and spoke in a voice low with menace. "You laughin' at me, puke?"

"No, sir!"

"Don't sir me, puke! I'm your platoon sergeant, an' I ain't no sir. Only *officers* is sir. You got that?"

"Yes, sir!"

"*Jees-us*! Did I say *brains*? They teach you English there in college, boy? They teach you how to fuckin' un'erstan' English?"

"Yes!"

"Yes, *what*? gawdamnit!"

"Yes, *sir*!"

"*Omigod*!"

Shaking his head, he had marched us off into a completely alien world. Quantico was first and foremost a hostile place. We were petitioning for membership in an elite fraternity, and those already accepted plainly didn't want new members. There were more candidates at that time than the Marine Corps needed second lieutenants, with the result that four companies in the training battalion were ranked in status by both staff and students in terms of which produced the fewest graduates. Our lieutenant, who was only a year or two our senior but who stood apart as one who had made it, let it be known that his ambition was to wash out his entire platoon. We were constantly being urged to DOR

(Drop at Own Request). Although the most visible tool for weeding out unsuitable candidates were tests of physical endurance, there were more subtle psychological pressures which were at least as effective.

At OCS all the signals which in growing up we had subconsciously learned to use in adjusting to the world around us suddenly went haywire. One of the more dramatic aspects of this nightmare was the breakdown of visual associations. Clothes and haircuts, in those days at least the most visible clues in the instinctive process of sizing up new aquaintances, no longer served either to shore up our own identities or to give any clues about the people around us. Despite wearing similar uniforms and being herded around like cattle, we all felt isolated and completely naked before the all-seeing eyes of our omnipresent sergeants. For them we could do no right.

"You like me, candidate?"

"Yes, sergeant instructor!"

"I can't hear you, candidate!"

"Yes, sergeant instructor!"

"Well, ain't that nice! You queer for me, maybe?"

"No, *sergeant instructor!*"

"Well, let me tell you something, college boy. I don't like you, an' I don't want no peckerhead like you bein' my officer an' gettin' my ass killed, so why don't you just DOR an' go home to momma so's I don't have to *make* you DOR, which is just what I'm gonna do. You got that, boy? I'm gonna fuck all over you till your ass is hangin' so low it's got worms crawlin' in it. Now, you gonna DOR?"

"No, *sergeant instructor!*"

"*Shit!*"

The most important thing in our lives became to win the respect of those sergeants. Plainly, nothing we might have considered as accomplishments prior to coming to Quantico counted for anything in their eyes. Going to college, which for most of us was our proudest achievement up to that point, apparently won us only the scorn of our new mentors. We were playing now by their rules, so it had followed that their ways became our ways and their standards became our standards. In ten weeks they made us over into their own image.

They orchestrated this transformation with the subtlety of instinctive psychologists. "Tomorrow," warned our gunnery sergeant, "we is goin' for a little walk on the Hill Trail, an' ain't none o' you maggots that's got balls enough to stay with me." Of course most of us stayed with him, and when we did we felt we had done the impossible. We waited for his "well done" after we won the obstacle-course competition. Instead he took us on a three-mile run. The day we graduated he came storming into the barracks at 0430, just as he had the first day we got there. "Git outside!" he bellowed, and in five minutes we were in uniform and formed up on the parade deck. I looked around at the former philosophy majors and engineers who now stood ramrod straight, and I remembered the laid-back sophisticates who had straggled off that train just ten weeks before.

The gunny surveyed us with disgust. "What do you peckerheads call yourselves?" he growled.

"*Marines!*" we roared. I suppose even then some of the more cynical among us realized how cleverly the Marine Corps had turned us around, but even those who did were yelling just as loud as everyone else. And even today, with many of my friends from those days killed in a bungled war, I still get shivers up my spine when I hear the Marine Corps Hymn, and I remember that moment at OCS with no less pride. So it was no coincidence that much of my thinking about my new school was colored by the things I had seen work at Quantico.

As had OCS, I wanted to start by creating an environment so different from the one delinquent kids had grown up in that none of the attitudes they had learned on the street would any longer apply. I guessed, correctly as it turned out, that street kids measured their effectiveness by their success at crime, and I hoped I could be as effective with them as our sergeants had been with us at undercutting their pride in their previous accomplishments and giving them a new set of standards to measure themselves against. Recalling the moment I had stepped off the train at Quantico, I saw the value of making the transition between their old world and the new one I would plunge them into as abrupt and dramatic as possible. Ideally this school of mine would catapult its students into a society where honesty ranked above deceit, self-reliance above preying on others, and compassion above the ability to inspire fear.

There were some things I didn't want to copy from OCS. Quantico had the mission of training essentially peaceful people to be violent. We would be in the opposite business. Our job would be to break down the association that existed in our students' minds between violence and physical toughness. Consequently the sarcasm and ridicule that our sergeants had used to such good effect would have no place in a school intended to reform delinquents who were probably already all too familiar with these mannerisms in their dealings with each other. I sensed that few kids in trouble would ever have had the chance to develop healthy friendships with adults and, while I wanted whomever I found for staff to be as effective role models as our DIs had been, I saw no reason why this couldn't be done in a more friendly way.

Although the goals I contemplated sounded innocuous enough when written down on the innumerable lists that I was churning out at the time, I wondered if even these wouldn't put my students into an emotionally vulnerable situation more complex than perhaps I was competent to deal with. Any attempt to change their behavior would have to begin by discrediting most of the perceptions and values they would bring with them. Convincing a boy whose idols were bullies and con men that such people were scum would be to undermine his whole conception of manhood. The attitudes he had grown up admiring were obviously the ones that led to status on the street. By trying to introduce him into straight society I would be breaking down the accommodation to society that he had already made and asking him to play by rules that might even earn him the ridicule of his peers.

In the moments of doubt that increasingly began to beset me as my school advanced along the path from dream to reality, I wondered more and more if the boot-camp/Outward-Bound model I was developing would be enough, by itself, to do the job.

3

U NTIL THIS POINT I had spoken of my plans to very few people other than my wife, Yara. She had been quietly encouraging, and only much later did I realize how close to heartbreak she had been as she listened patiently to my enthusiastic monologues.

Yara was born in the northeast of Brazil at a time when her father had been a rising star on the Faculty of Law at the University of Fortaleza. The Brazilian northeast was then still a wild, brawling place similar to our own West of a hundred years ago. While Yara was a very young girl, the governor of Fortaleza had embezzled public funds and then blamed a subordinate for the missing money. Although the legal community had all deplored this state of affairs, the only one among them who had the courage to risk the governor's displeasure by defending the wronged man was Yara's father. He won the case but lost his job and had to flee with his family to Rio to avoid further retribution from the authorities.

In Rio he was driven to justify the hardship he had brought on his wife and children by espousing increasingly quixotic causes which met the test of his principles but did little for his pocketbook. He opposed the succession of military dictators that ruled Brazil, and poor Yara grew up with the mortification of watching this wonderfully impractical man ignored or ridiculed at the street-corner rallies where his message of dissent was feared and his patrician manner resented. As to the generals in power, they considered him too eccentric to be dangerous, but they nonetheless made sure he was barred from any but the most humble faculty positions. Consequently his family lived in poverty, supported mainly by the meager profits from a music school his wife started, where Yara herself taught piano from the age of nine. The only bright spot in this unhappy story was that her musical training had led to a scholarship at the Juilliard School in New York. We met in 1969 while I was teaching at the Naval Academy, where she had taken a summer job in the Language Department.

In 1973 our second son was a year old. We had bought a house in Woods Hole, and with my Marine Corps pension along with my salary from the Oceanographic, we were getting used to the luxury of an adequate income. It never occurred to me what it would mean for Yara to lose the security represented by a regular paycheck. While I was growing up the few times my own family was strapped for cash had seemed more like adventures than hardship. Yara's childhood, by contrast, had taught her all too well the real meaning of poverty. She bravely bit her lip while I pontificated about the evils of a system that locked men into jobs they hated with the insidious fetters of pension plans and seniority benefits. All the while she was hearing the voice of her own father saying the same kind of things as she and her mother worked to put food on the family table. On the day I came home to proclaim that I had given notice at the Oceanographic, Yara smiled gamely. Later I noticed a sudden increase of piano students around the house.

I'm ashamed to admit that I was too elated at my new-found freedom to be much conscious of Yara's concerns or worried by the financial implications of the course I'd embarked on. I faced for the first time in my life the heady prospect of running what would be entirely my own show, and my first concern was with how to organize the effort. I had experience with two management models: the rigid command structure of the Marine Corps, and the more informal administration at the Oceanographic. In practice neither approach had worked quite as I had expected. The Marines had been self-conscious enough about leadership to make it the subject of formal study. Those endless lectures we had yawned through at Quantico while it was being drummed into our heads that a leader could delegate authority but never responsibility had translated in the field into a system that, when it worked as it should have, gave even those of us well down the chain of command pretty much free rein within the limits of our jobs and held us accountable only for results. While in college I had accepted with worldly scorn the conventional stereotype of the inflexible "military mind." So it had come as all the more of a surprise to find myself a humble second lieutenant with more responsibility than was common among my classmates who remained in civilian life.

When I arrived at Woods Hole, the scientists I met at the Oceanographic called their leaders "administrators," a term which suggested simply paper shuffling without any of the moral or inspirational ingredients of leadership. Management was regarded as an unpleasant necessity, reluctantly undertaken by men whose inclinations lay elsewhere. With the same logic that led the Navy to entrust the command of aircraft carriers to aviators with limited experience at ship handling, the Oceanographic reserved its senior administrative posts for scientists who were novices at management. Among this group even those who had transferred into administration early in their careers still maintained the myth that theirs was just a temporary interruption from more meaningful work in the lab. Because they didn't consider leadership as a profession in itself, few gave much thought to their roles. Some were so uneasy with command that they put popularity ahead of effectiveness. Others became so infatuated with their positions that they refused to delegate even the most trivial decisions. In both cases the end result was inefficiency. Decisions requiring quick action, even if on the basis of incomplete information, were often catastrophically deferred for further study by former investigators whose training had left them oblivious to the importance of timing in management. Decisiveness was somehow seen as ungentlemanly in a community of scholars, and the resulting ambivalence about "power" fostered an environment that hid a good deal of friction and fumbling beneath its relaxed facade.

As I grew more familiar with the Oceanographic, however, my skepticism about science management was tempered by the suspicion that among scientists a certain amount of laid-back fumbling might be psychologically more important than administrative efficiency. The beards and eccentric costumes that were so much a part of the lab reflected a vaguely defined commitment to anarchy that I began to realize would have made the staff balk at a structure in which those Marine Corps leadership principles were more self-consciously applied. I wondered if the same would be true with the group from which I planned to draw my prospective staff.

Structure of any kind was not much in vogue anywhere in 1973, and this was particularly so in Woods Hole, which had become something of a Mecca for a group of Establishment dropouts who had grown restless in their careers and were looking for more fulfilling alternatives. Some among these free spirits lost their bearings midway between occupations and ended up wandering aimlessly about in overalls, but most had been more clear-eyed in their decision to trade security for work they could be proud of. All were idealistic enough to believe that by redirecting their own lives they could help to change that part of the national character that was responsible for Watergate and for what were perceived to be our sins in Viet Nam. Collectively these rebels represented a reservoir of great talent but prickly sensibilities. Altruistic, unconventional, committed to living in harmony with nature, and hoping to work with both their hands and their heads, they seemed ideal for the sort of staff I was looking for. But they were also so skeptical of anything even resembling organization or "power tripping" that I wondered if they would be willing to run a tight enough ship to stay on top of volatile kids in an accident-prone environment. I also wondered whether they would work for me.

Given the sentiments of my prospective colleagues, the trick for me would be to come up with an organization loose enough to accommodate antiauthoritarian sentiments while still retaining the benefits of a system that encouraged initiative and held individuals to account. Ideally a school designed along these lines would function as a partnership of friends, each one with responsibility for the success of a defined piece of the pie and answerable as much to his own conscience as to me for how well he did. My job, first and foremost, would be to find the right people.

Everything about the Massachusetts Department of Youth Services (DYS) I was reading at the time stressed the use of professionally trained "clinicians" to staff the emerging system of community-based private programs for rehabilitating delinquents. Psychology majors were well enough represented among my pool of prospective staff so that I didn't think I'd have much trouble finding people with the appropriate credentials, but I wasn't convinced that the type of therapy offered by someone who thought of himself as a clinician was the best way to influence delinquents, at least not the kind of former delinquents I had known in the Marine Corps. My own childhood spent in a family and at a school where the privacy of one's feelings was respected to the point of almost total inhibition made me more than a little prejudiced against the kind of soul-baring that seemed to be the basis of the "clinical" approach to rehabilitation. For one thing it just seemed too public to ring entirely true.

Newspapers and magazines were filled with poignant accounts of troubled young people "working through their problems" with the help of benign, bearded therapists wearing earrings. Perhaps this "let-it-all-hang-out" attitude was no worse than the kind of reticence I had grown up with, but even then I wondered if these clinical outpourings of feeling weren't becoming a kind of game in which self-infatuation passed as self-awareness or in which broad-mindedness masked a feeble reluctance to judge between right and wrong. My suspicions were reinforced when I came upon the absurd spectacle, photographed in a national magazine, of a bloated therapist reduced to tears at the contemplation of his own obesity and being comforted by his delinquent charges. Somehow I doubted if such things really happened.

I had grown up trying to be like the adults I admired. How, I wondered, could any kid admire an overweight therapist weeping tears of self-pity? Besides, the whole scene smelled of fraud. Could that lugubrious fellow actually have been weeping crocodile tears to show those kids they weren't alone in their problems? Wasn't what we were seeing a transparent piece of theater concocted to establish a climate in which the therapist and his charges would, in a mutually "supportive" way, learn to "feel better about themselves" by swearing off pasta and hot cars? Christ! I doubted if even Private Johnson would have played that game.

If that passed as therapy, then I wanted nothing to do with it. What I wanted for my staff were role models, not fellow sufferers.

If I was going to be teaching carpentry, fishing and farming, why shouldn't I look for carpenters, fishermen and farmers who could be the kind of examples I remembered from my own childhood?

But then another recollection from Quantico knocked me off this high horse. At OCS there had been a lot of emotional injury unintentionally inflicted by officers and NCOs who had been insensitive to the vulnerability of the candidates they were evaluating. My students, no less than those at OCS, would be putting their self-images on the line. The most insecure kids would probably have the biggest emotional stake in their macho identity, just as the least qualified candidates usually had been the ones who most needed the image represented by the Marines. I didn't know how street kids would react to threats to their identities, but I knew that many of the candidates who had been hounded into dropping out of OCS saw in their failure a reflection on their manhood that left deep scars. My carpenters, farmers and fishermen might inadvertently do the same damage to the boys they were trying to help. Without professional training, did we have the right to mess with kids' heads?

As an instructor at OCS I had lobbied for more selectivity in assigning staff to the training companies on the grounds that we had a responsibility to minimize as much as possible the potential for emotional trauma in the necessarily cruel business of weeding out the unfit. Picking only "good Marines" for staff had not been enough at OCS. Nearly everyone assigned there was a good Marine, but some were better judges of character than others. The best were the ones who would back off before they had stripped the broken candidate of his last vestiges of pride. They were not, however, easier task masters. Instead the same sensitivity that led them to stop short of destroying a recruit's last emotional defenses also made them better able to spot the bullies and blowhards who too often slipped through a system that was somewhat unfairly weighted in favor of the big and the fit. With such types, who were often harder to break, they were ruthless.

There was no correlation between those who had this particular kind of sensitivity and their rank or education. One of the most perceptive Marines I knew was Gunnery Sergeant Shank, who had been my DI when I was a candidate. Gunny Shank was a taciturn, raw-boned mountain man who was somewhat miscast as a drill in-structor, since he lacked the sense of theatrics the job called for. He plainly felt uncomfortable working with "college pukes," but he took seriously the job of preventing incompetents from becoming officers in his beloved Marine Corps, and his quietly genuine disgust when we fell short of the mark made him in my eyes just as effec-tive as his more colorful counterparts. We called him Old Rawhide.

We had in our platoon a frail boy named Winget whose father had been killed on Iwo Jima and who, I suspect, had been driven by this fact toward a career he wasn't any too well suited for. Winget had all the courage in the world, but he lacked the stamina to keep up on the forced marches that were the most brutal source of at-trition at Quantico. Day after day he would stagger along until he collapsed, all the while refusing to DOR, and finally there had come the dreaded call to the battalion office, where Winget was told that if he failed one more march he would be dropped.

The next morning our company fell out in the pouring rain for a hike along the infamous Hill Trail. We were the last platoon in the order of march, which was bad luck, since despite constant calls to "close it up," men all along the column would sag back and then have to double-time to catch back up again. The farther one was toward the rear, the more pronounced would become the ef-fect of this accordionlike progression, until the last platoon was running all the time. I was assigned that day to Gunny Shank's stretcher bearers, whose job it was to follow in the trail of the com-pany to pick up stragglers, and as I moved to my position in the rear I noticed that the gunny had moved Winget to the head of the column.

Then the command *move out* came echoing down the line fol-lowed by *double-time,* and the company lunged like a great clank-ing green serpent at the first of the endless, slippery, red-clay hills that lay ahead. Almost at once men started falling out, but Winget hung on. At the five-mile mark I saw him begin to stagger, as one by one the men behind him began to pass him up. Our lieutenant fell back with him, verbally flailing him on, but still he lagged until somewhere around the sixth mile he fell for the last time and could go no farther.

The lieutenant, who was never one to pass up the opportunity for theatrics, stood over Winget shouting contempt, while we stretcher bearers shuffled awkwardly about, and the gunny looked on in disgust. "Shit," he spat. "You candidates get the hell outta here!"

I set off with the rest of the stretcher bearers after the fast-receding company, but the gunny called me back. As I turned around I saw him grab the lieutenant by the arm and say something I was too far away to hear. Whatever it was, the lieutenant stopped his tirade open mouthed and went scuttling off after his platoon. Then Old Rawhide, who never had a good word for anybody, knelt down beside the sobbing Winget and said simply, "You done real good, son. You gave it all you got, an' there ain't many of us as can say that."

We carried Winget back to the truck, and the next time I saw him he was standing in a formation of other failed candidates waiting to go before the Battalion Fitness Board. He alone in that dejected group still held his head high, and I knew when he grinned at me that thanks to Gunny Shank he would survive that humiliating experience with his pride intact.

I never forgot that brief moment on the Hill Trail. Gunny Shank had done something almost magical back there. Winget, with his dream in ruins, had been wide open, and the lieutenant would have left him with a burden of shame he might have carried for the rest of his life. The same intuitive quality that had enabled the gunny to avert that tragedy was what I wanted in my staff, and the more I thought about it the more convinced I became that this quality was inborn. Some men had it, others didn't. I didn't believe the kind of intuition I was looking for had anything to do with clinical training.

This suspicion was based on an experience I had had when, nine years after leaving OCS, I was ordered to the teaching staff at the Naval Academy. There to my disgust I found that the Navy, whose business was supposed to be leadership, entrusted the teaching of this subject to civilian psychologists. Nonetheless I listened to what these authorities had to say and had to admit that it all made sense. But even after acknowledging the value of "positive reinforcement" and the like, I still left their classes with the vague feeling that something was missing in the idea that leadership, like typing, could be presented as an acquired skill, available to anyone who mastered the simple principles involved. Granted, those experts had done a good job of breaking leadership down into its component "techniques," but nothing they were telling those midshipmen could explain Gunny Shank's magic. Our lieutenant had measured up well enough against the standards of the classroom. What he lacked, and what no one could teach him, was the gunny's instinctive sense for other men's feelings that could tell him when to bear down and when to back off, when to praise and when to demand more. The lieutenant's leadership came from his head, not his heart. We knew he was playing a role, just as we knew the gunny was not. Old Rawhide wasn't applying any carefully learned methodology to whip us into shape. If he hadn't been entirely unaffected in both his disgust and his praise, his illiterate tirades would have made him a buffoon rather than the role model he so effectively was.

Would delinquents be any less perceptive than we had been at OCS? I doubted it. If we had smelled fraud in an officer who led by "technique," wouldn't a kid be equally suspicious of a therapist who attempted to modify his behavior through the mere application of some learned method? If I were the boy I had just read about in yet another starry-eyed article, who had just belted his therapist, I would be damn confused when my victim's response was to offer to "talk through the reasons for my hostility." Even if I decided to play out this charade all the way to a well-orchestrated reconciliation, I doubt if I could have convinced myself that my emotions were for real. Probably, though, I would have tried. Those group sessions and role-playing games, and all the other exercises in sensitivity, had a kind of appeal to them. I imagined that even the most cynical street kid was really lonely enough to accept this kind of ritualized "caring" as a substitute for the real thing, even while his instincts were rebelling against it. Perhaps the warnings from his inner self would be too incoherent for him to understand the reasons for his uneasiness, or maybe he would balk consciously at the thought that the people who said they cared about him were being paid to do so. Either way something would be telling him that what he was feeling wasn't genuine, and so, I suspected, the whole experience would roll right off his back once he was on the street again.

What bothered me equally about the textbook approach to leadership and the clinician's approach to rehabilitation was that both catered to the shallower side of human nature. The inducements they offered to promote the kind of behavior they sought were essentially bribes aimed at showing that there was less effort and more pleasure in following the approved path. But neither leadership nor rehabilitation had anything to do with taking the easier way. Leadership meant inspiring men to voluntary self-sacrifice in the name of some greater purpose, even if the greater purpose was usually no more abstract than loyalty to the man beside you. Rehabilitation involved teaching a kid to follow the dictates of conscience rather than expediency. How could you persuade a boy from an environment where thievery plainly paid off that it would be in his best interest to stop stealing? You might convince him that it would be to his immediate benefit to stay straight, but as soon as the odds for successful crime turned again in his favor, wouldn't he logically go back to his old ways? The thief remains potentially a thief until he is deterred from theft by his conscience rather than by the fear of jail.

My students would need some higher motive as an incentive to honesty when, as their own experience confirmed, honesty didn't pay. My concept of rehabilitation had nothing to do with the non-judgmental efforts to help a kid "get in touch with his feelings" I had been reading about. Instead, weaning a boy from delinquency had to involve the self-conscious effort to instill in him a code of honor strong enough that he would make the meeting of its standards the measure of his own self-worth. The only way I could think of to do this was by example. Wouldn't kids just naturally end up adopting the values of people they admired? I thought they would.

So I ended up by coming a full circle in my thinking. The same reasons that had led me to doubt whether I should attempt to do what I was trying to do without the help of professional therapists ended up by confirming my original preference for a staff whose professionalism would be in the trades and skills I intended to teach. If the kids we would be working with were the same kind of kids I had met in the Marine Corps, they didn't need therapy.

They needed the example of adults who embodied the same qualities we hoped to foster in them. They were vulnerable, in the same way that Padgett had been vulnerable, but the tough veneer they hid behind was not likely to be penetrated by clinicians practicing techniques learned in the classroom. A better approach would be to treat them as decent human beings normally treat one another. If their behavior called for anger, they needed adults who would get angry. If they did well, they deserved the praise of men they admired. If they were hurt, they needed someone who would help them as Gunny Shank had helped Winget. More than anything else, they needed role models who, like the gunny, were the genuine article.

David Masch was in Antarctica when I wrote to ask him if he would be interested in helping me start the school. Since the *Gosnold* cruise, he and I had gone our separate ways. The invisible barrier between scientists and administrators having once again reasserted itself, we did little more than say hello on the infrequent occasions that our paths crossed, but from what little I had seen of David, I sensed that he was a real Pied Piper with young people. A frequent scene during summers in Woods Hole was of David, festooned with poles, nets and pails, leading processions of urchins off clamming or fishing. In the evenings he ran the village teen center, and I suspect he deserves credit for shepherding a number of local young people through the difficult period when drug abuse in Woods Hole reached almost epidemic proportions. He was inseparable from his own son, with whom he engaged in elaborate schemes to outwit the authorities while poaching herring.

David grew up in Detroit in a strict German Lutheran community, some of whose members had looked askance when he departed for the fleshpots of Cambridge with a scholarship to Harvard. Four years later he confirmed the suspicions of his critics by refusing to return home to a respectable job, and chose instead to knock around at various Bohemian pursuits before landing in Woods Hole, where he quickly established a reputation as one of the community's foremost cooks and gardeners.

When I first arrived at the Oceanographic, I saw evidence of David's skill at gardening in the form of an enormous pumpkin displayed on top of a very tired old Volkswagen. From listening to what was being said by the crowds who gathered to marvel at this monstrosity, I gathered that its owner, who turned out to be David, was displaying it to discredit innuendos concerning his abilities which were being circulated by disgruntled losers whose produce he had found wanting while serving as vegetable judge at the local agricultural fair. His culinary feats were no less remarkable, and invitations to his dinners were much coveted and often later regretted by the distended diners who staggered away from his table.

David had an imposing presence which concealed a gentle soul. Over the years that I have known him he has mellowed a bit, but in 1973 he was still a very vocal critic of the capitalist system, which his studies of ocean food chains had convinced him was criminally wasteful of the world's resources. His somewhat defensive belligerence in expressing this opinion, along with his baleful stare and sarcastic wit, tended to intimidate strangers. Among his friends, however, he was known for his endless repertoire of funny stories, his love of good books and good conversation. In his youth his eye for the ladies had occasionally led him into difficulties, but by the time we met he was in the process of being brought firmly to heel by the powerful lady who became his second wife.

On the *Gosnold* cruise David had impressed me with his unselfconscious competence in the practical arts of the fisherman and marlinspike sailor. At night when we assembled sleepily on the floodlit fantail to bait up the long line, he worked twice as fast as the rest of us. During the day his large, capable hands proved equally adept at the delicate art of scrimshaw. Even then, before we had become friends, I decided he was one of those kinds of people who might occasionally be irritating in small matters but who would always be there when it counted.

David was a lot less threatening to young people than to adults. He got along equally well with the little people he took fishing and the world-weary teenagers at the Village Center by communicating with both groups without artifice or condescension. I hoped my letter would find him in a receptive frame of mind.

While waiting to hear from David, I set about trying to recruit Herman Bosch. Herman had run away to sea at seventeen. He crewed on freighters in the Pacific during the last days of World War II, eventually working his way up through the merchant-marine ranks to third officer before coming ashore to get his Ph.D. in oceanography at Johns Hopkins. It was a source of some pride to him that he was perhaps the only doctor of philosophy in the world without a high-school degree. He was afflicted with an astronomical IQ, and like many super-intelligent people, suffered from an incurable restlessness that kept him moving between places, wives and careers. The one constant in his ever-changing life was his love of teaching. He could explain anything to anybody.

I met Herman because I coveted his boat. My own boat at the time was lying at a slip opposite his, and I used to see this weather-beaten character coming and going in a pretty little trap boat called *Sagitta*. Although my school was then a vague dream, and I hadn't yet found an island to put it on, I knew I would eventually need a boat, and *Sagitta* looked like what I wanted. Herman, it turned out, had recently become disenchanted with doing research at the Marine Biological Laboratory and was in the process of setting himself up as a commercial fisherman. He had taken as a partner a former philosophy major named Mike Collins, and the two of them had bought a very tired old Stonington dragger named *Amrial*, with which they hoped to make their fortune. Mike, whose inscrutable expression earned him the nickname of Chinaman, went on to become a high-line fisherman, but at the start neither he nor Herman knew enough about the practical aspects of the trade to make their venture a success. Herman was not accustomed to failure in any of his myriad pursuits, so he plugged valiantly on, but every time I saw him climbing dejectedly out of *Amrial's* foul bilge I would say something about my school, and eventually I noticed his ears beginning to prick up.

I also mentioned my scheme to Tom Aldrich, an accoustical engineer at the Oceanographic who, to my surprise, immediately offered to help out. Tom didn't have the security of the independent income I had from my pension. As planning for the school proceeded and it became increasingly apparent how financially shaky a venture we were getting ourselves involved in, he reluctantly, but sensibly, concluded he couldn't support his family on the uncertain salary he could expect from our school. During a time when I would otherwise have been entirely on my own, however, Tom's unflagging enthusiasm helped me weather the many periods when I was overcome with doubts about the wisdom of what I was trying to do. He never worked at Penikese, but he played a large part in getting the school started.

The first thing Tom and I did together was to get in touch with the Department of Youth Services. A call to Boston revealed that DYS was organized into seven regional offices, each one of which had its own director who was responsible for the department's affairs in his particular part of the state. Cape Cod fell under the jurisdiction of the Region VII Office, which was located at the time in Taunton. I phoned Region VII's assistant director, Jack Haywood, who suggested we come up to see him. So Tom and I drove up to Taunton where, in a dingy suite above a run-down store on the main street, we found his office. Climbing up a flight of graffiti-lined stairs, we passed a couple of tough-talking, long-haired boys in the company of their defeated-looking mothers and entered a desk-filled room decorated with posters showing soaring seagulls, waterfalls and the like, beneath which were inscribed inspiring profundities such as Today Is the First Day of the Rest of Your Life. Somebody had crossed out "day" and written in "fucking."

This was my first encounter with the oppressive combination of sights, sounds and smells that I have since come to associate with all the institutions that deal with crime. Graffiti, vandalized toilets, peeling paint and an atmosphere heavy with cigarette smoke, sweat, fear and hopelessness are the ingredients common to every probation office, jail, police station and court building I have ever visited. That Taunton office owed its decrepitude as much to age as to its occupants, but even those new steel-and-glass showcases built as monuments to the Great Society's conviction that crime was among the social problems that could be buried under an avalanche of dollars soon succumbed to the same blight, their defaced splendor providing, if anything, an even more stark reminder of the failure they represented.

So I had a vague feeling of uneasiness as we were ushered into the presence of Mr. Haywood. The man we met was a pleasant bureaucrat whose firm handshake and florid features suggested an ex-jock now enjoying a little too much of the good life. He was one of the few veterans at DYS who had survived the purges that had marked the department's recent history under Jerome Miller, and his mix of macho with the jargon of the clinician showed the nimble balance of the born survivor.

"You gotta care a lot to make it in this business. I'll tell you now, I'm gonna throw some tough kids at you just to see if you can take it. You think you can handle that?" We said we thought we could, and, that established, Mr. Haywood went on to describe the mechanics of submitting a proposal to the Department of Youth Services. "Programmatic approval" for our school would have to come from DYS, following which our budget would be scrutinized by a watchdog agency known as the Rate Setting Commission, whose job it was to protect the Commonwealth's financial interests in any contracts between public agencies and the private sector. If all went well on both fronts, we would be awarded what was known as a Purchase of Service Contract, in which our operating costs would be divided by our enrollment to arrive at a daily cost per student. We would bill the Commonwealth at the end of each month for the number of boys actually enrolled and could expect payment four to six weeks later. New programs, Mr. Haywood advised, would do well to come up with a rate low enough to attract referrals. Asked what constituted a competitive rate per student, the assistant director suggested $20 per day.

We, in turn, briefly described our own proposed program which, as we then envisioned it, would involve a series of six-week courses involving boat building, survival and seamanship training for classes of eighteen teenage boys. "Sounds good!" he enthused. "Let me know when you're ready, and I'll send you the kids."

"Jesus," said Tom as we drove home. "How does he know we're not a couple of perverts?" I assured him that DYS would certainly investigate our motives and backgrounds more thoroughly before sending us the kids. They never did.

The next day we set out in earnest to find ourselves an island.

4

THE FIVE ELIZABETH ISLANDS stretch westward from Woods Hole to form a fifteen-mile-long chain which separates Buzzards Bay on the north side from Vineyard Sound on the south. Naushon, the easternmost and largest of the five, is followed by Pasque, Nashawena and Cuttyhunk, with Penikese, the smallest, lying a mile north of Cuttyhunk.

Although Leif Ericson is thought to have sailed among the Elizabeths, the first recorded landing by Europeans was made on Cuttyhunk by Bartholomew Gosnold in May of 1602. From Cuttyhunk Gosnold sailed over to Penikese where he stole an Indian canoe, thus becoming the first delinquent to visit that island.

The Elizabeths in Gosnold's time were heavily wooded with cedar, beech and oak. Most of these trees were later cleared for pasture, and today the islands are largely windswept stretches of barren grass and scrub. On Naushon there remains, among the only stands of virgin timber spared the axe, a huge beech on which Ralph Waldo Emerson established another unfortunate precedent by carving his initials.

In the midnineteenth century Naushon, Pasque, and Nashawena were acquired by the Forbes family of Boston, who by and large allowed these islands to return to their natural state. By 1973 Cuttyhunk, with a year-round population of about fifty people and a fair-sized summer colony, retained the only permanent settlement of any size left on the Elizabeths. The last resident had left Penikese in 1941.

Several weeks before our first meeting with the Department of Youth Services, I had written to the trustees of the Forbes family's conservation trust to ask permission to set up our school on Pasque, which of the three privately owned islands seemed the one best suited for our purposes. Pasque lies west of Naushon and is separated from it by a twisting channel known as Robinson's Hole. The island served during the American Revolution as a refuge for Tories forced to flee the mainland and is the site of what may be the oldest house in Massachusetts. At the time I wrote, Pasque was occupied only by Freddy Gaskell, the reclusive, solitary caretaker, whom I did not then know well enough to realize how much he would have resented having our company. Freddy lived in one of the complex of buildings on the east end that once housed the exclusive Pasque Island Fishing Club. There is a probably unfounded story to the effect that the wealthy sportsmen who fished out of Pasque used to communicate with their brokers via homing pigeons. Whether the story is true or not, I still can't pass Pasque without conjuring up images of frantic executives scanning the horizon for the birds carrying news of their fortunes.

A hard current scours through Robinson's, and there is only a small lagoon, impassable except at high water, on the island itself. Getting on and off Pasque in a boat of any size could be precarious, but it seemed to me that this disadvantage was offset by the island's proximity to Woods Hole and by the fact that it was not actively used by its owners.

The Forbes family trust gave my request fair consideration before turning it down on the grounds that granting us access would establish a precedent for admitting other users who, no matter how worthwhile, would collectively detract from the trust's objective, which was to keep the islands forever wild. I had to agree with the family's contention that in the long run public interest is served by keeping some parts of the world free from the public. Still the decision was disappointing, since I could have no school without a place to put it. But why, Tom Aldrich suggested, did we need an island? Couldn't we accomplish our objectives using some of the undeveloped land at the largely abandoned Otis Air Base only fifteen miles from Woods Hole?

That thought had never occurred to me. The Hurricane Island Outward Bound School in Maine had inspired my first notion for a school, and the proximity of the Elizabeth Islands had made it seem achievable. Right from the very beginning the idea of an island had been central to the whole scheme. Now I had to ask myself how important an island location really was to what we were trying to do.

In retrospect the arguments for the necessity of an island that I marshaled in opposition to Tom's suggestion were colored more than a little by my own romantic attachment to the idea of recapturing the ideal of a simpler outdoor existence that island life represented. More practically, however, I remained committed to the concept of creating the same kind of abrupt transition between worlds that OCS had so effectively subjected me to, and I could think of no better way to do this for a group of urban ghetto kids than to pack them into a boat and ship them off to a remote, uninhabited island. No land-based wilderness location arrived at by car or even on foot could possibly provide so dramatic a break with the past. "The program we are developing," I had advised DYS, "is intended to introduce the student to an environment so different than the one he is accustomed to that the responses he has developed from earlier experience will no longer provide the results he expects."

Arguing the advantages of islands, however, could not change the fact that we didn't have one. Cuttyhunk, with its relatively large population, was obviously out of the question. Among the Elizabeths, that left only Penikese, and Penikese didn't look any too good. It was twelve miles from Woods Hole. Access by boat was no easier than at Pasque, particularly when hard southeast winds blew directly into the shallow bight that provides Penikese's only sheltered anchorage.

Surprisingly for the smallest and topographically least interesting of the Elizabeths, Penikese had the most colorful history of the lot. From 1642 until Civil War times the island was inhabited by farmers and fishermen, some of whom had served as pilots to vessels entering Buzzards Bay. There remains atop Penikese's highest hill a well-worn boulder shaped roughly in the form of an armchair where John Flanders, a famous pilot and wrecker during the early 1800s, sat waiting to pilot the ships which would accept his service, and to salvage those which wouldn't.

In 1867 a wealthy New York tobacconist bought Penikese and, six years later, donated the entire island, along with a substantial sum of money, to the famous Harvard naturalist, Jean Louis Agassiz. Agassiz's dream was to establish a school where his students would "study nature, not books." The John Anderson School of Natural History, named in honor of the donor, opened in 1873 and became the forerunner of the scientific laboratories later established in Woods Hole. Agassiz's school was also innovative in being coeducational. This raised eyebrows at the time and even led to the writing of a musical comedy suggesting that other natural activities were also investigated on Penikese. Photographs from the period show a number of impressive buildings with gingerbread trim in use by the school.

The enormous job of founding his school and overseeing the construction of its elaborate physical plant, all of which was done in only four months, broke Agassiz's health. He died in December of 1873, leaving the island school to limp along for another year under management of his son before it closed its doors forever. Penikese reverted to the ownership of John Anderson, whose heirs later sold it to a New Bedford turkey farmer.

Leprosy meanwhile was becoming a widely publicized health problem in Massachusetts. The disease had come to the state with the waves of immigrants then arriving from Russia, the Azores and the Orient. In 1905 the state Board of Charity, thwarted by popular opposition to its plan to open a leper colony in Brewster on Cape Cod, acquired Penikese Island for this purpose. Doomsayers predicted that ships would no longer dare to approach Fall River or New Bedford due to fear of contagion, but the Board of Charity pressed on regardless. Some of the old Agassiz school buildings were converted to a hospital and quarters for the staff, while cottages for the patients were built on the windy west side of the island. A ten-thousand-gallon cistern was dug next to Agassiz's two smaller ones atop Penikese's highest hill, and water, pumped up from wells dug in the valley below, was gravity fed to the lepers' cottages. On November 18, 1905, five patients, banished by law to live for the rest of their lives apart from society, arrived on Penikese to be met by the newly appointed superintendent, Dr. Louis Edmonds.

The leper colony's first years were marked by hostility among patients of differing ethnic backgrounds and low morale among the staff, who found themselves pariahs whenever they returned to the mainland. Momentary excitement caused by Dr. Edmonds' announcement that he had cured one of his patients was followed by even greater gloom when his diagnosis proved to be in error. Edmonds resigned in despair and was replaced on January 1, 1907, by Dr. Frank Parker as superintendent and Mrs. Parker as matron.

Dr. and Mrs. Parker were extraordinary people. He had given up a successful medical practice, and she had abandoned her home in Malden, Massachusetts, to come to Penikese, where they were to spend the next eighteen years of their lives with less than three weeks off the island during the entire time. Their many friends had labored mightily to dissuade them from what was considered certain suicide, but the Parkers would not be stopped. The energy and good spirits they brought to their dispirited patients transformed the small colony almost overnight. Men and women who had formerly spent their days in forlorn idleness soon were planting gardens and actively farming the island. Dr. Parker lifted the ban that had restricted patients to the west side of Penikese, and Mrs. Parker organized parties and church services. Men of God, reluctant to accept Mrs. Parker's invitation to minister to her charges, were tartly advised to believe that "the Master will take care of you, and if you haven't got faith you are out of your place."

The patients confined to Penikese had adapted with varying degrees of success to their unhappy fates. Some exploited the Parkers' boundless kindness, while others were incoherently grateful. "I am sorry very much," wrote an elderly Greek, "because I cannot repay that help you did for me." Adversity brought out the best in some and the worst in others. Even Dr. Parker, who could find no ill in anybody, eventually lost patience with a recalcitrant Turk whom he described, in his only recorded criticism of a patient, as a "disturbing element." In contrast to this "unfortunate addition to the Colony," there was Archie Thomas and his equally gallant mother. Archie was sixteen when diagnosed as a leper. Mrs. Thomas had caused a sensation by deciding to accompany her stricken son to Penikese. "Braves Living Death for Love of Son!" had trumpeted the *Fairhaven Star* in one of the many lurid articles that brought unwanted fame to this poor woman. Archie's hobby as one of the country's first ham radio operators also attracted national attention. Mrs. Parker found him a radio with which he provided his fellow patients a welcome window to the outside world.

The Parkers' house burned down during a January gale in 1912, destroying everything they owned. Archie Thomas died three years later and was buried in the small west-end cemetery attended by his friends, many of whom were soon to follow him. Spirits undaunted, the Parkers carried on until 1921, by which time leprosy had been brought well enough under control that the hospital on Penikese was closed and its remaining patients transferred to the federally operated leprosarium in Louisiana. A crew of daredevils from New Bedford were hired to dynamite the buildings on the Island, with the thought that so doing would kill any remaining leprosy germs, and ownership of Penikese was transferred to the state's Division of Fish and Game, who maintained a caretaker there until 1941 when Penikese was declared a bird sanctuary and abandoned. Dr. and Mrs. Parker retired to Montana after Massachusetts refused to grant them a pension.

Agassiz's ill-fated school, the sad fate of the lepers, and a further tragedy involving the accidental shooting of the caretaker's grandchild led a local historian to brand Penikese "The Evil Island." But evil or not, it was the last of the Elizabeths that remained as a possible site for our school, so Tom Aldrich and I went down with our families one early spring day to have a look at it. We landed alongside the falling-down stone jetty that had once led out to a long-gone wood pier and made our way along an abandoned road leading up a hill to a grove of sumacs. Kicking through the long grass, I stumbled over an iron manhole cover, which we lifted up to reveal a still-intact well. A nearby concrete foundation contained evidence that it must once have been a pump house, and more poking around uncovered four more wells, all filled with good water. Farther up the hill stood the nearly collapsed ruins of the caretaker's cottage, beyond which was the beautiful cut-stone foundation to Anderson's barn. Broken concrete and twisted metal were all that was left of the dynamited hospital.

On top of the island's eighty-eight-foot-high "mountain" we found the ruins of the three cisterns, the two of brick largely destroyed and the one of concrete still in pretty good shape. Nearby was a bronze plaque which had been set into a granite boulder in 1923 to commemorate the fiftieth anniversary of Agassiz's school. The site was well chosen. Standing there, I could look eastward along the Elizabeth Islands to Woods Hole. South and only a mile away stood Cuttyhunk, beyond which I could see Gay Head on the west end of Martha's Vineyard, and beyond that, barely visible in the haze, was Noman's Land. Eleven miles to the north, the stacks of New Bedford stood above the skyline, and westward, beyond Fall River, I thought I could just make out the arch of the Newport Bridge.

We wandered over to the west side towards the still-standing walls of what had been the lepers' steam-fired laundry and the overgrown ruins of their cottages. Caved-in cellar wells were filled with old iron bed frames, chamberpots and bottles. Long-ago-planted daffodils still pushed up from stone-bordered flower beds. Beyond sight of the cottages was the little cemetery where I found the headstone of Lucey Peterson, whom Dr. Parker had described as "pretty and well formed" when first she arrived on Penikese.

The sun was setting by the time we headed back down towards the pier to board Dick Edwards' surplus Coast Guard buoy tender which had brought us down to Penikese, and which, in the years to come, would make countless more trips to the island to carry everything from lumber to tractors. At that time, however, we were still unfamiliar with the many shoals around the island, so we felt our way out slowly towards deep water in the gathering darkness. To the east the nearly submerged rocks of Gull Island shone in the light of the setting sun. Our sleepy children were roused momentarily by the sight of a harbor seal before succumbing for good to the soporific throb of the diesel. Once we cleared Gull Island, the fathometer showed good water, and we headed for home, steering on the loom of Nobska Light.

On March 28, 1973, I wrote to Mr. James Shepard, director of the Massachusetts Division of Fisheries and Game, to request permission to establish our school on Penikese Island. My letter led to an interview with Mr. Shepard in the course of which Tom launched into a euphoric description of his vision of happy children dancing around the campfire on Penikese. At this the director looked a bit puzzled, since the image plainly didn't square with his impression of how to treat punk kids. I must say that I, too, had a bit of trouble picturing those sullen boys we'd seen at the DYS Region VII office in Taunton innocently dancing around the campfire. It looked for a while as if Jim Shepard was going to write us off as a pair of naively idealistic dogooders, and I frantically tried to disabuse him of this impression by stressing the similarities between our proposed program and Parris Island.

Mr. Shepard was immediately receptive to our request but saw two obstacles in the way of granting it. The first was legal. Penikese had been declared a sanctuary by legislative act, and a ruling from the Massachusetts attorney general would be required to determine if the use we proposed could be considered compatible with the act's intent. The second problem was political. Fish and Game's mandate was to promote the interests of hunters and fishermen. Consequently the division's wildlife-management policies sometimes drew fire from the state's most influential conservation group, the Massachusetts Audubon Society.

The director agreed with our contention that limited occupancy of Penikese by responsible people would enhance the island's value as a sanctuary by stopping incidents of vandalism and poaching which the Cuttyhunkers had been complaining to him about. He was not sure, however, if the Massachusetts Audubon Society would see things in the same light, and he was quite frank in saying that this was not an issue he wanted to risk an altercation over. It would therefore be up to us to convince Audubon of the merits of our plan.

The staff of Massachusetts Audubon proved to be a thoroughly professional group of people and a far cry from the image of hysterical alarmists that developers and exploiters attempt to attach to conservationists. Dr. Ian Nesbit, at that time the society's chief ornithologist, was an English physicist whose interest in birds had developed from his work on highly sensitive radars. He had been using migratory flocks as difficult-to-detect targets and found himself becoming more interested in the birds than the radar, whereupon he took up a new career. Dr. Nesbit's long battle to protect natural habitats from encroaching civilization made him less than enthusiastic about the prospect of our occupying one of the state's last uninhabited sanctuaries, but he nonetheless agreed to visit Penikese to assess the damage I alleged was being done by unauthorized visitors.

On the day we were to meet in Woods Hole I found myself without a boat to get to Penikese. My own was too slow, and Dick Edwards' boat was off doing something else, so I went to see Dan Clark, our local marine contractor, to see if I could borrow something from him. Dan does everything in a big way. Rather than lend me a boat, he summoned up Norman Gingrass' seaplane, and a few minutes later he, Dr. Nesbit and I had landed on Penikese and were crawling through a thicket of rose bushes counting baby night herons. Ian scuttled about like a ferret with Dan's huge figure following in his wake and me bringing up the rear. Every time one of us would spot a nest we would all gather silently around the little featherless creatures within it, Ian's face a study in professional concentration, Dan trying not to laugh out loud at the absurd-looking birds and me hoping the little buggers wouldn't mind too much having us for neighbors.

From the rose bushes we proceeded to the old stone walls to search out the nests of the Leach's storm petrel. Penikese is the southernmost known rookery for these little black seabirds, and Ian worried about how the nesting colony would react to human presence. On the other hand there was no ignoring the evidence that Penikese, unoccupied, was being badly abused by poachers and vandals. Graffiti, trash and spent shotgun shells littered the island, while a large patch of burned-off grass behind the pier provided testimony to the danger of fires.

As we moved about, clouds of herring gulls rose shrieking from nests packed so closely together it was hard to avoid stepping on them. Ian was explaining how the exploding gull population had crowded out the terns that used to nest on Penikese when Norman landed in the cove to pick us up. We left with Ian candidly undecided on whether to recommend for or against our occupancy of Penikese.

But even though the day hadn't brought an unqualified endorsement from Massachusetts Audubon, the trip had served to win the school the support of Dan and Norman, both of whom were to be instrumental in the equally important job of winning the support of neighboring Cuttyhunk. Dan Clark stands nearly seven feet tall and has a long white beard, which makes him look like a Cecil B. De Mille portrayal of God. He lives in a house built from the timbers of ancient vessels, where on winter nights colorful characters assemble around a roaring fire to tell sea stories and drink great quantities of rum. Woods Hole folklore abounds with tales of Dan's generous nature and colossal feats of strength.

Norman Gingrass, who died in 1987, was a laconically unflappable Yankee who was equally a legend in his own right. He had come to Woods Hole to fly for the Oceanographic and left that job to start his own seaplane service among the offshore islands. Over the years his yellow seaplane had become a familiar sight along the coast, and tales of his skill were passed around whenever islanders got together. For years, while feeling my way along in thick fog, I often heard Norman passing close overhead or else found him taxiing nonchalantly off Cuttyhunk waiting for the momentary lift in visibility that was all he needed to get off the water. Sundays on Penikese usually began with the roar of his Cessna passing at chimney height and the thump of an air-dropped newspaper hitting the porch.

As with many remote communities, small incidents tend to develop into long-standing feuds on Cuttyhunk. Dan Clark is one of the few people who is on good terms with all of the island's several factions, and so, while waiting for a decision from Audubon and the attorney general, I went back to Dan to ask how to proceed with the ticklish business of enlisting the support of our prospective neighbors for the idea of importing delinquents to Penikese. True to form Dan dropped what he was doing to call Norman, and off we flew once again, this time to pay a call on Cuttyhunk's deputy sheriff, Dave Jenkins. The deputy sheriff proved to be a man of few words. He allowed as he couldn't see much wrong with having us on Penikese, particularly since delinquents couldn't be any worse than the poachers who already overran the island. We flew home, and I thought no more of Cuttyhunk, which turned out to be a foolish mistake.

Ian Nesbit, meanwhile, was wrestling with his conscience. Massachusetts Audubon was then researching the concept of multiple land use on the theory that the remaining wilderness areas in the Northeast might better resist pressure for development if they could be used also, without damage, for socially valuable activities which were compatible with the natural environment. Since our proposal might provide a test case for one such activity, the society agreed to give its qualified endorsement to locating a wilderness school in a sanctuary area. The attorney general also ruled in our favor. On July 12 Jim Shepard of Fish and Game gave us the go-ahead, on terms that our occupancy of Penikese would be subject to continued monitoring to ensure that we were not degrading the island's value as a sanctuary.

This was followed by a small article in the *New Bedford Standard–Times* to the effect that the state had decided to build a prison on Penikese. I was unaware of this bombshell until Dan Clark called to report that the citizens of Cuttyhunk were about to meet in emergency town meeting. No sooner had Dan hung up than the phone rang again, this time with poor Jim Shepard on the line wondering why furious Cuttyhunkers were calling for his head. I was babysitting our oldest son, George, at the time, so the two of us ran down to Dan's and, for a third time, flew off with Norman to Cuttyhunk.

We arrived at the little white frame building that serves as the Cuttyhunk town hall to find the atmosphere heavy with tension. The only face I recognized among the crowd was that of Selectman Alan Wilder, the caretaker on Nashawena, whom I had met earlier through Dan. Alan was justifiably annoyed that I hadn't said anything to him about my plans, but nonetheless very decently spoke of me as a friend in his introduction to his constituents. Then angry silence fell over the crowd as I launched into a fumbling defense of my school which was punctuated with hostile questions from the floor.

"What happens when they grab your guns and take over the place? What's to stop them from coming over here?"

"These are kids, Ma'am. We won't have guns."

"Kids, hell! I've seen those kids. You better have guns."

"No, Sir. I've seen them too. We won't need guns."

"Yeah? I've been reading about you guys. Bunch o' goddamn bleeding hearts. What those kids need is a good kick in the ass, if you'll pardon the expression. Not a bunch o' you peacenik psychologists."

"Well, I'm no psychologist. Most of my ideas for this school came from what I learned in the Marine Corps."

"So why don't you just send 'em off to the Marine Corps? We don't need 'em here. That's for damn sure."

So it went. The tide of public opinion was clearly not swinging in my direction, and to make matters worse, I could see little George beginning to plot mischief from his front-row seat. Then the one man unpopular with just about everyone present rose unsteadily to his feet and launched into a drunken lament for the geese and herons that would be left homeless if we displaced them from Penikese. Since this man was a notorious poacher, the irony of his remarks was not lost on his audience who set up a chorus of coughing. Unfazed, my critic droned on while I waited, unaware that his interminable speech was doing more for my cause than I ever could.

George, meanwhile, was contemplating Alan Wilder's huge plastic hardhat which lay on the corner of the stage. Finally he could stand it no longer. Just as our speaker was winding himself up to a peak of incoherent indignation, my son raced from his seat to put on that hat. He had not, however, reckoned on its enormous size. The helmet engulfed all of him but his feet. And so, bewildered by un-expected darkness, George went bumbling unsteadily off looking like a drunken turtle, with me in pursuit. The crowd broke up into gales of laughter.

Thanks to George there were a lot more friendly faces in evidence when we left the hall. Cuttyhunk wasn't happy at the prospect of having us as neighbors, but at least the town was willing to give us a chance.

5

BY MIDSUMMER 1973 we had $20,000 in hand from two foundation grants and little immediate prospect for more. Although we had not initially planned to involve kids in building the dormitory on Penikese, it occurred to us then that a good way to get to know our future students and to generate the additional money we needed would be to start in the fall of 1973 with a reduced enrollment of ten of DYS's more responsible clients, who would help us ready Penikese for occupancy the following spring.

Jack Haywood at Region VII was enthusiastic about this idea. I reminded him that we would be in a hell of a financial fix if he didn't send us the ten kids and in equally great trouble if he sent us the wrong ones. "No problem," he assured me, "We'll get you some good kids."

And so we began. The school's first student arrived on the island on August 28, 1973, and moved into the already overcrowed tent city we had set up beyond the beach. The arrival of two more kids and several million horseflies a few days later made it plain we would have to devise more permanent living arrangements until the house was built. Dan Clark came to our rescue with the loan of his eighty-five-foot coastal freighter, which we moored in Cuttyhunk Harbor and moved aboard. *Nereis* made the round trip to Woods Hole every other day, usually with a couple of boys aboard, to shower, do their laundry, and sleep in a real bed at one of our houses.

In mid-September Dan's barge, loaded with seventy tons of building materials, arrived in Cuttyhunk Harbor after trying unsuccessfully to get into our own shallow anchorage. For the next fifteen days *Nereis* shuttled back and forth moving this material across to Penikese. The job of unloading the barge brought home to us how much support we had from the town of Woods Hole. It seemed as if everyone who had a way to get to Cuttyhunk came down to man the fleet of improbable boats laden with impossible loads that plied the waters between the two islands. Our students, now numbering six, began to get caught up in the spirit of the effort.

The last load went across to Penikese on the third of October, and then began the job of hauling the mountain of material up the hill to the building site. The prospect of moving the whole pile all over again seemed so enormous that the kids' morale flagged. We got our work force going again by specifying each morning the material to go up the hill and telling them that once finished they could have the rest of the day off. No matter how large the load we assigned they were generally done and swimming by midafternoon.

Architect and construction foreman for the house was my former *Gosnold* shipmate, Dr. Peter Laue. Peter was a bit of a hermit and preferred living by himself in a roofed-over root cellar on Penikese to commuting from Cuttyhunk. We arrived early one morning to shake the good doctor out of his bed and found an inscription neatly carved above his door advising that The Place To Be Is Where You Are.

"That's crap," remarked one of the kids indignantly. "What if you're in jail?"

Our students were by now over their initial culture shock and were finding their own individual niches in the small society that was developing on Penikese. Duane, the first to arrive, was a wiry, sandy-haired boy of fifteen who was fascinated with all things mechanical. Whatever the gadget, he had to learn how it worked, and this generally meant taking it apart. Rarely did the object of Duane's curiosity survive his investigations, with the result that he left a trail of destruction behind him. Although he had been diagnosed as too hyperactive to function in school, he seemed to find on Penikese an outlet for his restless mind and unlimited energy. He absorbed new information like a sponge, worked furiously at projects he enjoyed, and objected equally furiously when he didn't get his own way.

Duane had a long record of violent assaults on teachers and anyone else who "crossed" him. He lived alone with his elderly widowed mother who alternately requested the state's help with her uncontrollable son and then made a great show of protecting him from the caseworkers who attempted to intervene. Despite his protestations to the contrary, Duane was plainly proud of his ability to terrorize people. He claimed to "throw a nutty" when angry and denied any recollection of his violent behavior after he calmed down. We once caught him torturing a wounded gull and found that he could be equally brutal with some of the more vulnerable kids. All of this made us wonder if there wasn't at least some element of premeditation in his "nutties." All in all, however, Duane's darker side surfaced relatively infrequently on Penikese. Most of the time he was just a high-spirited boy who loved boats, living outdoors, and taking things apart.

Nick, also fifteen, was a girlishly handsome boy who had been involved in numerous arsons . His penchant for lighting fires had made us uneasy about bringing him to Penikese, particularly since Duane, who knew him, reported admiringly that he was unbeatable at the test of courage then in vogue among DYS kids, which involved two boys' allowing a cigarette to burn down between their clenched forearms. The loser flinched first.

We had been persuaded, however, to accept Nick on the strength of the department's opinion that his fire setting "seemed more the product of circumstances than [of] his own inner dynamics," and it did seem as if our fears had been ungrounded when we met the cheerful, outgoing boy who arrived on Penikese early in September. Nick talked openly about his past problems and his determination to solve them. His hope was to set an example for his kid brother and spare his mother further unhappiness. We were so impressed with his candor that we put him in charge of the petty-cash box.

Danny, who was sixteen, was the third boy to arrive at Penikese. He had been abandoned by his parents as a small boy and had grown up as a ward of the state in a series of foster homes from which he was in the habit of running away. He came to us from the department's well-run Homeward Bound Program, where his instructors had expressed the hope that, for this "consummate mama's boy," further physical effort "would gradually temper his mind and body into a more reliable functioning organism."

Nothing during Danny's first weeks on the island gave us much hope that we were contributing anything to this tempering process. It seemed that his unhappy childhood had entirely drained him of spirit. In contrast to other kids, all of whom suffered from a surfeit of misdirected energy, Danny could sit numbly for hours doing nothing. Although he was not a bad-looking boy, his features along with the rest of his body seemed somehow unformed. His only motivation was to be liked by his peers, and they, sensing this, could lead him into the most degrading activities which he would carry out woodenly in hopes of winning friendship. Instead he earned only their contempt, which further contributed to his confusion and unhappiness. Danny was basically a shy and gentle boy, not well suited for life at Penikese; but at least he found there freedom from the pressures that had forced him into degrading sexual behavior on the street.

Jack and Bill were both sixteen and both came from Fall River, but there the similarity ended. Jack was as close to my image of an "old-fashioned delinquent" as ever came to Penikese. A feisty little Irishman who rolled drunks to support his mother and sisters, he had been roaming the worst streets of the city since he was eleven. Jack was both the kindest and the most fearless of our kids. He alone among a group of instinctively selfish boys would never go for coffee without asking if someone else wanted some too. He was so lacking in artifice that his spontaneous generosity was never suspect, even to the other kids (who were always suspicious of ulterior motives). Nothing so outraged him as injustice. Any unfair division of labor would drive him into such a comical fit of incoherent indignation that nobody could stay angry for long. He loved animals and was much puzzled that the Almighty should allow little gulls and rabbits on Penikese to die miserably of starvation. "God," he concluded sadly, "must have fucked up."

Bill, who looked much older than his sixteen years, was our only student from an affluent background. His successful stepfather, with whom he didn't get along, saw in Bill evidence of the inadequacy of his wife's former husband, and Bill did little to disabuse him of this impression. He was disruptive at home and a failure at school. Perceiving himself a misfit in both places, he had found on the street a retreat where his physical strength was respected and his academic failures did not count against him. Despite his record of armed robberies, we began by thinking that Bill's middle class background would make him the least committed of the group to criminal behavior, but his boastful pride in his "record" soon disabused us of this impression. His "war stories" about holding up gas stations successfully one-upped Duane, whose proudest exploit was attacking a policeman with a harpoon. Poor Danny listened wide-eyed to these tales of derring-do. His own concocted tales of violent crime were laughed to scorn by the others until we banned all further "war stories" from conversation. But the spectacle of our least delinquent kid wanting desperately to be as "bad" as his more criminal companions made us wonder uneasily if there might not be something fundamentally wrong with the concept of trying to reform a delinquent in the company of his peers.

Stan was a big, good-looking seventeen-year-old who had dropped out of school and had a record of violent conduct when drunk, which was his usual state. He was generally sullen, showing little interest in anything but rather pathetically soliciting praise for whatever efforts he did make. His free time was spent in drawing skulls, motorcycles and daggers.

Pete, sixteen, who was our only private referral, arrived voluntarily later in the fall to escape an impossible home situation. Although he was no scholar, his comparatively normal childhood had put him so far ahead of the others in terms of general knowledge that his presence highlighted the startling lack of cultural awareness among the others. Of the DYS kids, all but Danny had tested out in the "dull-normal" range of intelligence. Although they had been promoted to "age-appropriate" grades by school systems anxious to be rid of them, their actual academic level was below the third grade. Jack didn't know the days of the week, and Bill couldn't read. Danny, a scholar by comparison to the rest, had once set out to walk to Florida. After walking all day and still not getting there, he turned around and came home.

Their written records and our first impressions of them had so prepared us for a group of dullards that we were properly humbled when Duane beat us all at chess. Bill mastered pinochle in one evening and amazed us with his ability to add scores in his head. Jack learned slowly, but once he managed to absorb a piece of information he didn't forget it. Even Stan showed occasional flashes of insight suggestive of an intellect beyond "dull normal."

So one of the most pleasant discoveries that first fall was that we were dealing with kids who were every bit as quick as any randomly chosen group of straight kids of the same age. Their dismal performance on the battery of "psychologicals" they had all been subjected to seemed more an indictment of the tests than an accurate reflection of their abilities. Another pleasant surprise was that behind hard faces still hid little kids. Boys like Jack had had to be street tough for so long that they had been cheated out of childhood. But more and more often as they grew used to island life, their hard veneers would peel away, and we would find them whooping and romping like a bunch of Huck Finns.

As fall wore on and the days became shorter, what for the kids had begun as an adventure began to look to them more like rugged, cold work. It became harder to get them going in the morning and harder to keep them going on the job. War stories resurfaced. Duane treated us to occasional "nutties," and Nick fell victim to disturbing mood swings. Matters came to a head one cold morning when the two of them refused to go to work. Danny, who could always be counted on to align himself with the most negative influences around him, joined this sit-down strike.

The two staff on duty found themselves with the same Hobson's Choice that so often still confronts their successors today. What should take precedence, work on the island or work with the kids? If they had spent the morning browbeating their recalcitrant charges into action, Peter Laue would be left alone on Penikese, and winter would be one day closer without progress on the house. On the other hand, leaving the troublemakers behind on the Frenchman, which seemed the only alternative, didn't look like too good an idea either.

The right solution would have been for one staff to take *Nereis* across to Penikese with Jack, Bob and Stan while the others remained behind. But we were all novices then, and getting that house up had become an obsession. So both staff and the three non-mutineers set off for the island, leaving Duane, Nick and Danny alone on the Frenchman.

We learned what happened next from Duane and Danny. It seems that during the morning Nick's behavior became increasingly "weird." He first began pulling burning logs out of the stove and brandishing these around his head. Danny, by then thoroughly scared, started whimpering about fire, at which point Nick went after him with a kitchen knife.

"Hey! Cool it, man!" yelled Duane, causing Nick to turn on him. There were a couple of tense moments before Nick put up the knife and began ransacking the boat for anything of value he could find. The petty-cash box yielded $70 which he offered to share with the other two if they would run with him. They refused, and Nick hailed a ride ashore from a passing boat in time to catch the ferry to New Bedford.

When the crew returned that evening they found two very scared kids and no Nick. Somewhat sheepishly they called in this news to me in Woods Hole, and I in turn notified the appropriate people at DYS, thinking as I did so that after so great a screw-up as this one the future of the Penikese Island School was none too promising. To my relief, however, no one I talked to at DYS seemed particularly surprised or upset. So many DYS kids were on the run in 1973 that another one hardly mattered.

The following day I drove up to the city where I tracked Nick down to a seedy-looking apartment occupied by some equally seedy-looking older men. These gentlemen piously urged Nick to mend his ways, and Nick, with equal earnestness, expressed shock and consternation at his own behavior. "Honest, George-man. I dunno what made me do it. Jeez, after all you guys done for me. . . ."

We returned to his house to pick up his clothes, and while Nick went into the bathroom to change, I played with his three-year-old brother. The two of us were rolling his ball back and forth when suddenly and for no apparent reason this little boy, who moments before had been laughing happily, flew into a violent rage and bit me in the leg. Nick, meanwhile, had made his escape out the bathroom window. The boys' mother didn't seem much upset about either development.

As I drove home, I could almost hear my old first sergeant bellowing "born bad," and I was haunted once again by the spectre of Private Johnson.

6

WHENEVER A PENIKESE KID "bombs" dramatically there inevitably follows a kind of catharsis during which the rest of the gang reacts instinctively with a sense of "there but for the grace of God go I." Such was the mood after Nick's departure. Dinnertime "war stories," which we had come to recognize as a barometer of prevailing attitudes, again faded from conversation. Fights were fewer and faces more cheerful. Without being able to say so, the kids seemed to recognize that together we were building something worth saving. Jack in particular was so pathetically desperate for even the fragile stability provided by our temporary little community that he would look at his former friend's empty bunk and shake his head. "Dumb shit!" I overheard him mutter, "What'd he run for? Fucker even told me he liked it here."

All the kids took possessive pride in "their" house, which under Peter Laue's supervision went up surprisingly fast. On November 9 we raised the roof with appropriate ceremony, and by the end of that month the building was entirely closed in.

Relations with DYS, meanwhile, were proceeding less smoothly. Within a week of leaving Penikese, Nick was picked up on new charges following which his caseworker called to ask if we would take him back. We put this question to the other kids, who were plainly uncomfortable at being consulted. Loyalty to their former colleague, or perhaps fear of him, made it difficult for them to turn him down, but averted eyes and shuffling feet indicated that much was being left unsaid. We were still too inexperienced to recognize their mute appeal for protection from Nick, who they knew would force them back into their street roles.

We still believed no kid was beyond our ability to save. So we agreed to give Nick another chance, on terms that DYS first lock him up for two weeks in order to demonstrate to him and to the other kids that bad behavior led to bad consequences. His caseworker objected to this approach as being "punishment oriented" and took us to task for "rejecting" Nick. We knew, however, that the rest of the gang was watching carefully to see how we would react to the first major violation of our honor system, so we stood firm on our conditions, much to the annoyance of assistant director Haywood.

DYS allowed Nick to remain at home, where in due course he set fire to another house, which led to the death of a fireman. Bill, our sea lawyer, raised a point we found hard to rebut. "What the fuck, man. We bust ass all day to stay on this freezin' island. Nick splits, and they let him go home."

The department's unexpected response to Nick's fall from grace brought home to us how little we understood the rehabilitation system of which we were now a part. We knew little of the bitter political struggle that led to the closing of the old state training schools, and we understood little more about the philosophy of Jerome Miller's followers, who had recently come to power in DYS. We had accepted, without any firsthand information or experience, the reformers' contention that the training schools had been a bad thing, and we shared their belief that rehabilitation was an achievable goal. We knew they intended programs such as ours to be alternatives to locking children up, but we didn't realize that even for kids like Nick they had ruled out incarceration — or any other form of real punishment.

DYS's rejection of punishment as a matter of principle was a legacy of the controversy that had raged around the question of "locking up kids" during the late 1960s. In Massachusetts the crusade against the training schools had been fought as part of a larger movement that sought to eliminate the practice of segregating troubled children, the mentally ill and the physically handicapped inside the network of aging red-brick facilities that, ironically, had been created by equally ardent reformers of an earlier age. These once-imposing schools and hospitals, which had won Massachusetts national recognition as a pioneer in the field of social services in the early twentieth century, had become the target of a new generation of reformers who accused their predecessors of trying to hide rather than help the Commonwealth's more disturbed or disturbing citizens. Like most crusaders, the proponents of "deinstitutionalization" had refused to see any good in the system they fought to replace. State-run institutions were portrayed as lice-ridden warehouses. The people who staffed these decrepit facilities were branded as patronage appointees, perverts and sadists.

Attacks on the training schools were particularly vitriolic. Militant activists, using techniques learned from the antiwar movement and led by the charismatic Jerome Miller, who was DYS commissioner from 1969 to 1973, mounted a well-orchestrated campaign to expose the alleged mistreatment of delinquents. Influential liberal lobbies had taken up the cause, and the tide of public sentiment against the old system had risen to a point where most politicians recognized that any public defense of the training schools, which had long served them as convenient sources of patronage positions, would be suicidal. The training schools were closed. Miller's disciples purged the upper levels of the DYS administration of nearly everyone associated with the old regime, and Miller himself departed for a job in Illinois on a wave of national publicity. Only after he left did anyone notice that he had been more effective at closing the old system than at designing a new one to replace it.

Miller's successors at DYS shared his belief that adolescents in trouble could be voluntary participants in their own rehabilitation if given the chance. They saw the delinquent as a victim, driven to criminal behavior by external factors beyond his control, and this perception made the idea of punishing him unfair as well as unproductive. By this reasoning the training schools, no matter how humanely run, were immoral because they served as an instrument of the establishment, locking up children for crimes for which society itself was responsible.

The proposed solution to all the evils ascribed to the training schools was to treat society's unfortunates within their own communities. Miller's dream was for a network of privately run drop-in centers and halfway houses, all drawing on the support of their surrounding communities and staffed by dedicated, academically trained professionals skilled at treating the kinds of problems that would bring troubled adolescents trooping voluntarily to their doors.

The training schools had been staffed largely by Boston's own "good old boys," who owed their jobs in many cases to the same local political connections that had gotten their friends appointments into the police and fire departments. Outgoing, mostly macho types who were not averse to roughing a kid up a bit if he deserved it, the former training-school staff members I met through Penikese were nevertheless a far cry from the ogres portrayed by the reformers. A salty training-school graduate who later came to Penikese contrasted the old system with the one that replaced it pretty well when he said of his old instructors, "Those guys were OK. Sure, they'd slap you around some, but at least with them you knew what you had to do."

In contrast to their predecessors, Jerome Miller's protégés were young college-educated liberals dedicated to the belief that virtually all behavioral problems were malleable to therapy. Many of them affected the speech and dress of the counterculture and viewed delinquent behavior as a legitimate protest against an unjust society. The leaders among them moved on Miller's heels directly into administrative positions at DYS, where their lack of management experience soon created havoc. Worst of all they proved unable to fit the various convictions they had fought for into a coherent policy designed to accomplish the department's mission. Training schools were closed before adequate alternatives were in place for their former inmates. The mechanisms created to screen and fund private contractors were so inept that new programs were born and died like flies, often with large sums of money disappearing in the process. By renouncing punishment and abolishing detention facilities, DYS found itself powerless to deal with the unexpectedly large number of delinquents who, like Nick, rejected the department's help and continued undeterred in their lives of crime.

By the time Penikese came into being in 1973, DYS's credibility with the courts, the police and the general public had just about bottomed out. The same legislation that had abolished the training schools in favor of private alternatives had also stripped the courts of the power to confine juveniles directly. Children adjudicated delinquent in juvenile court might be placed on probation, in which case they remained under the jurisdiction of the court's own overworked probation department. For more serious crimes, they would be commited to DYS, which then became entirely responsible for their treatment. Lacking both the will and the means to confine habitual offenders, the department simply turned them loose again, with the result that it became not uncommon for the same boy to be committed one day and be back in court on the next to be recommitted for another crime. Street kids were quick to see that the system had no teeth, and before long juvenile courts developed a carnival atmosphere with salty young veterans laughing and shouting back and forth while police and judges ground their teeth in impotent rage.

The department's administrative credibility was no better. My increasingly impatient requests for the five more kids we had been promised to bring our enrollment up to the break-even point were met with evasive promises from Jack Haywood. After the incident with Nick, I was told that our refusal to take him back without an intervening incarceration had so outraged Region VII's caseworkers that they would no longer entrust their charges to us.

While all this was going on I was commuting back and forth from the juvenile court in New Bedford every time one of Jack's, Bill's or Duane's many still-outstanding charges came up for trial. The presiding justice, Howard Young, turned out to be an ex-Marine who liked what I told him about Penikese well enough to start recommending assignment to the island for the kids he committed to DYS. He could only recommend, however, and Region VII chose not to take his advice.

Whenever I appeared in his court, Judge Young would ask why his kids were not yet on Penikese. I would tell him that DYS hadn't referred them to us, with the result that we were nearly broke. At this he would fly into a great rage aimed at whatever DYS representative happened to be in earshot at the time. These tirades did little to endear Penikese to the unfortunate caseworkers who took the heat for their bosses' decisions, and relations with DYS were further strained when the judge summoned me and the director of Region VII to his chambers to find out "why kids aren't getting to Penikese."

Region VII at that time was the fiefdom of a crusty old politician named Jim McGinnes, the regional director, who had evidently been too firmly entrenched to be ousted by the reformers but who seemed quite happy to leave the running of the show to Jack Haywood, a decision he was later to regret when Haywood's mismanagement cost both of them their jobs. I had met him only once prior to this meeting with Judge Young. The director was heartily condescending to me and suitably deferential in explaining to the judge how His Honor must understand that the department's first priority in making placements must be the needs of the client rather than the financial status of a prospective program.

"Is that so?" thundered the judge. "Well, what about the Cabral boy I sent you for the fourth time last week. Father's a fisherman, kid tells me he likes boats. Why the hell isn't he suitable for Penikese?"

Mr. McGinnes had plainly never heard of the Cabral boy and so launched into some adroit backpedaling, which ended with the assurance that he personally would investigate the matter and see to it that Penikese got its full enrollment.

I expect he would have made good on his promise had not our ally, the judge, been relieved of his job shortly thereafter due to some alleged improprieties involving the use of his position for personal profit. Although I never learned the details of the chicanery he was charged with, I was sorry to see him go. Whatever his shortcomings, on the bench the judge was strict but fair, and he spoke a language the kids could understand. Among a pretty lackluster cast, he was by far the most impressive figure in the field of juvenile justice that I was to meet in 1973.

Region VII referred no more kids to us that year. As a result our income from the state in 1973 amounted to $5,000 rather than the $18,000 we had projected, and by the end of November it looked like Penikese would soon join the growing list of bankrupt DYS contractors.

The dilemma we faced was shared to a greater or lesser extent by every private agency that operated under a purchase-of-service contract. On the face of it purchase-of-service seemed perfectly fair. In practice the arrangement served to protect the Commonwealth at the expense of the contracting agency. The scheme was predicated on the assumption that an agency's costs were directly related to enrollment which, of course, they were not. Rent, salaries, insurance, etc., all remained constant whether or not the agency operated at capacity. Small, five- to twenty-client agencies of the size envisioned by the deinstitutionalizers suffered most from this type of contract, since the unexpected departure of even one client resulted in the loss of anywhere between one fifth and one twentieth of its operating income, until he could be replaced. For DYS-affiliated agencies, whose clients were prone to running away, this became a particularly severe problem.

The Commonwealth's fiscal practices further exaggerated the problems created by the contract. Reimbursement took so long that cash-flow problems were endemic among private agencies. Invoices were routinely rejected for the kind of usually inconsequential errors made by inexperienced program administrators, who were legitimately befuddled by absurdly complex accounting requirements. Massachusetts' reputation for delaying payments, a practice that began to look suspiciously premeditated, became so bad that most banks eliminated the contractors' last recourse by refusing to lend against the Commonwealth's unpaid invoices.

An even more serious fault was the fact that while the contract served to tie a program's income to its enrollment, it did not obligate the state to provide the program with sufficient enrollment to meet its expenses. If a state agency overran its own budget, it simply stopped sending clients to its contracting programs and left them holding the bag. This is what happened to us.

7

PENIKESE WAS SAVED from bankruptcy that first fall, as it has been many times since, thanks to the support of many good friends and the intervention of Boston's quietly influential network of private foundations.

Fred Mangelsdorf was my tutor on fund raising. Big-time philanthropy, he advised, was as far removed from old-fashioned charity as "horseshit from hamburger." Grantsmanship was a game derived from the now threatened piece of social engineering which made contributions to nonprofit organizations tax deductible. The Internal Revenue Service wrote the rule book. Donors made grants. Donees got them. Without one, you couldn't have the other, which is why, said Fred, aspiring donees such as myself should feel no awkwardness about asking prospective donors for money.

Fred had put me onto a giant tome entitled *The Foundation Directory* which listed every IRS-approved foundation in the country, along with the purpose and assets of each. In Massachusetts alone I counted 131 different organizations with combined assets totaling over $680 million. Nearly a third of them listed interests relating to youth, education or rehabilitation. With all that money out there, I figured it couldn't be too hard to get some of it.

Fred, however, had set me straight on the score by pointing out that most major foundations were staffed by experts in the fields they supported. These people measured their effectiveness by how efficiently they allocated the resources they controlled, and they were not easily impressed. The trick was to catch their attention. Competition for private money was so stiff that unsolicited proposals from unknown organizations were likely to fall through the cracks unless the petitioner had a friend in court. However, once a new enterprise got its foot in the door, things became easier. Foundations talked to one another, and support from one was likely to lead to introductions to others.

Fortunately for the future of Penikese, my friend Bill MacLeish, who was then editor of the Oceanographic's *Oceanus* magazine, was well connected in foundation circles and arranged an introduction for Tom Aldrich and me to Arthur Phillips, a trustee of the Cabot Foundation.

On the appointed day the two of us traveled up to Boston where we were met by Mr. Phillips, whose courtly manner could not hide his skepticism about the feasibility of the project we were proposing. The Cabot Foundation, along with many other philanthropic groups in Boston, was at the time being deluged with frantic appeals for help from newly founded programs and halfway houses in extremis due to late and inadequate payments from the state. Mr. Phillips knew better than we did the problems that beset these organizations, and he was quick to recognize that our budget reflected more wishful thinking than practical reality. He was also skeptical about our proposed location on an island, having seen other remotely based enterprises get in trouble because of the high cost of logistics.

On the other hand Mr. Phillips strongly supported what the human-service reformers were trying to do, and he recognized that the whole community-based experiment was in desperate need of new private programs if it was to have a chance to prove itself more effective than the old institutions. Torn between his instinct to warn us against an effort certain to lead to the same heartbreaks existing programs were already experiencing and his loyalty to a social cause he believed in, he prudently decided to compromise. His foundation would, he advised, consider making us a grant of $10,000, but only if we were able to generate commitments of enough support from other sources to give the school a reasonable chance of getting off the ground. He gave us the names of several other foundations that might be helpful and, as we left, suggested that I approach a well-known Boston surgeon, Dr. George Clowes, who summered in Woods Hole and whose family presided over a small foundation. Dr. Clowes was a great yachtsman and likely to be interested in anything having to do with boats. His opinions were well enough regarded in Boston philanthropic circles that his endorsement would carry weight.

Tom and I went home from Boston somewhat sobered by the gloomy picture that had been painted for us. Nonetheless I wrote Dr. Clowes, suggesting that perhaps we could meet in Woods Hole. I then succumbed to spring fever and decided to forget Penikese for a while and work on my sailboat. A few days later I was in the midst of gluing into place the pieces of an intricately fitted bulkhead when a stentorian voice thundered from the pier, "Lovely boat, that!"

The weather was unusually hot for April, my glue was setting up faster that it should have, nothing seemed to fit right, and I was having a hell of a time trying to prop pieces into position so I could screw them home. "Christ," I fumed to myself, "everything's turning to shit, and here comes some damn tourist wanting to talk."

"Umph," I grunted, in a tone that I hoped would end the conversation.

"You must be George Cadwalader," continued the foghorn, introducing himself as George Clowes.

Oh, my God! Forgetting that I was covered with glue, I leaped from the boat and gooily shook hands with the doctor. Just then my shakily propped up bulkhead collapsed with a crash, overturning the glue pot into the bilge. Yanking frantically to free myself from our well-cemented handshake, I dove once again into the boat, babbling incoherently about Penikese as I struggled like Br'er Rabbit with the Tar Baby to reassemble the pieces which now seemed to stick better to me than to where they belonged.

All in all, my performance that day was not one to inspire confidence, and so I was all the more grateful to the doctor when a few days later his foundation sent the newly incorporated Penikese Island School its first $10,000. This grant was accepted by Mr. Phillips as adequate evidence of additonal support, and the Cabot Foundation's check for another ten thousand soon followed.

Twenty thousand dollars along with the anticipated income from ten students for three months at $23 per day apiece, seemed like enough money to get started on, at least as soon as we could find ourselves an affordable boat better suited for all-weather operation than Herman Bosch's little *Saggitta*. There was a rumor going around the village that the Marine Biological Laboratory, which is Woods Hole's second major research center, was considering selling *Nereis*, its ancient but still sound thirty-five-foot collecting boat. So I went to see the MBL's general manager, Homer Smith, to find out if this was true.

Yankee that he is, Homer allowed as how the boat might be for sale if someone came along with the right price.

"What's the right price?" I asked.

"Dunno," said Homer. "Twenty-five hundred?"

"Jesus, Homer! We can't afford that. How about five hundred?"

To his credit he didn't throw me right out of his office but instead called Dan Clark to get a third opinion on a fair price.

"Sell her?" I heard Dan roar into the phone. "You skinflint, Homer, you know the Lab wrote that boat off twenty years ago! You ought to give her to George's school."

Homer put down the phone rubbing his ear. "One dollar," he growled. "Not a penny less."

I didn't have a dollar, so Homer contributed one to the school, and I solemnly gave it back to him to buy the boat.

A week later we had set up our tent city in the grassy clearing behind the old stone jetty on Penikese. David Masch built himself an outdoor stove from salvaged iron plate, while the rest of us set about mucking thirty years worth of trash and dead rabbits out of the wells. Duane and Nick arrived within a day or two of each other, to be followed soon after by our architect, Dr. Peter Laue, and Buck Buchanan, a mason Dan Clark hired at his own expense to help us rebuild the foundation for our future dormitory.

We were all at work one morning on these various projects when Herman Bosch arrived from Woods Hole to announce with theatrical pomp that, while circulating as was his habit among the rich and famous, he had met a wealthy summer resident who wanted to help us out.

"Yeah?" said Duane, putting down his hoe. "Ya think he'll help me mix this fuckin' cement?"

"My boy," intoned Uncle Herman, "you don't understand. My new friend has money. *Shitloads* of money. When a man like this talks of help, he's not thinking of mixing cement."

All work promptly stopped as we debated stratagems for relieving our prospective benefactor of his fortune. Duane's and Nick's suggestions about how this might be done were rejected as being too direct, and it was instead decided at Herman's urging that we invite him and his wife to dinner on Penikese.

Herman returned to Woods Hole to convey this invitation and radioed back later that afternoon that we should expect Mr. and Mrs. Philanthropist at six the following evening. Elaborate preparations were immediately set in motion. David went off to the cove with his clam rake to gather the ingredients for his famous quahog spaghetti sauce. Peter built a dinner table, and Chip Jackson, our naval officer-turned-artist, tutored the kids on appropriate topics of dinner-table conversation.

Throughout the following day David labored over his pots. Occasionally members of our cooking cognoscenti (of which I was not one) would be summoned to discuss how best to improvise around some missing ingredient. Scouting parties were dispatched to find wild garlic. Herman was enjoined by radio for chrissake not to forget the butter. In the growing tension it became necessary to institute a ten-pushup "fuck fine" aimed at sensitizing the community to the damage this ubiquitous word might do to our financial future if used at dinner.

Around five o'clock the chef was seen to smile, and we knew the crisis was past. Excuses were found to visit the kitchen, where we all gathered reverently around the stove to assay from a common spoon samples of the elixir that would secure our fortune. "Gentlemen," declared Dr. Peter solemnly, "we have here a sauce that would loosen the purse strings of King Midas himself!"

Herman came alongside the jetty promptly at six and, despite Fred's counsel against feeling awkward in our role of beggars, we made proper fools of ourselves bowing and scraping before our guest and his matronly wife.

David's dinner began triumphantly. As the full moon rose over the silver waters of our cove, we all sat down to a meal of superb spaghetti and genteel bonhomie. Then Duane, trying politely to make conversation with Mrs. Philanthropist, stuck his finger in the sauce and inquired, "Hey, this shit's fuckin' good, right?"

Shocked silence followed as all eyes swiveled in his direction. "Fuckin' forgot," Duane mumbled as he dropped down to do his ten pushups.

Nick saw from our guests' expression that something was amiss and rose to the occasion. "What they make us do," he explained, "is when ya say fuck ya gotta do ten pushups, which is why Duane's doin' em now."

"Yeah," he added with a grin. "That's how they bust our balls here. I bet Duane an' me's done a hunnert fuckin' pushups already today. It's the pits, man!"

At this, the pent-up energy generated by six people trying not to laugh was unleashed in a great shower of spaghetti. Buck bellowed, David wept, and the rest of us gagged and choked. Even dour Dr. Peter could only rock back and forth on his bench, slapping the table and chanting, "Jesus! Jesus! Jesus!"

Only Mr. Philanthropist remained staring stonily at his plate until at length our roars subsided into awkward silence. Then, looking pointedly at Peter, he reminded us that only the Lord could truly redeem sinners. What part, he inquired, would formal religious instruction play in our rehabilitation program?

David had suffered enough at the hands of stern Lutherans to be vitriolic on the subject of organized religion. I saw his face darkening, and so I jumped in quickly to say that while we hoped to teach Christian values we could not as the recipients of public money introduce school prayer to the island. Whatever the truth of this lame piece of improvising, it was met with such visible disapproval on the part of our guest that I began to suspect that our cause was lost.

I was right. Several days later we received a coldly polite letter of thanks and a check for $50.

Not all our benefactors were so unbending. One rainy afternoon aboard the Frenchman I heard the roar of an engine reversing frantically and a mighty clang as a boat smashed into our rough iron hull. I rushed up on deck to find a spry old gentleman nonchalantly tying up alongside.

"Never have got the hang of driving this thing," he explained. "Inboard-outboard, you know. Too complicated by half, if you ask me."

"Oh, well," he went on, surveying his topsides. "No harm done a little paint won't fix. Concordia built her for me. They know me over there, so they built her extra strong."

With that he hopped aboard and introduced himself as Oliver Loring. "But nobody over here calls me Oliver. They call me 'The Bishop'. Rather they didn't, really, but it's all right. I once was a bishop, you know, so there's no harm in it."

He was a bishop—the retired Episcopal Bishop of Maine—and in his own gentle way he was an indomitable little man. Along with Dan and Norman, Oliver Loring was one of the few people universally liked on Cuttyhunk, and on that first visit he offered to be our ambassador to the village.

"Oh, yes," he chuckled. "You've stirred up a regular hornets' nest over there, you and your bad boys. Well, maybe I can help. They all think I'm just a daft old man. They're entirely right, of course, but sometimes they do listen to what I have to say."

The Bishop—we called him that also—adopted Penikese with the same enthusiasm he had for anybody or anything he saw good in. He became our most ardent fund raiser, cheerfully hitting up anyone who appeared "to have more money than God intended." Over the next several months he and Mrs. Loring made many trips to the island from their home in South Dartmouth, and, if ever God guided a boat, He did theirs, since the Bishop never did "get the hang of it." Mrs. Loring's cookies, always delivered in a round tin box, were the only ones we ever conceded to be better than our own.

On one of their visits the Bishop came marching up the hill with a big sign saying Chapel on it, which he nailed solemnly to the outhouse door. Some of his most reflective moments, he explained, had taken place on the pot, so he felt the sign was appropriate, particularly since he had observed that some of our students spent much of the working day in the outhouse. Later, another visitor expressed outrage at our irreverent sign, and I took malicious pleasure in telling him who had put it there.

8

AS CHRISTMAS DREW NEAR and we prepared to close for the winter, the kids' talk at dinner turned increasingly to going home. Danny again listened wide-eyed as the other four tried to top one another with largely fictitious tales about their cars, their girlfriends and the good times ahead. It was all a bit sad. Their childhoods had in every case been nightmares, but the instinct that pulled them back to the scenes of their unhappiness remained pathetically strong. Home, however, was about the worst place possible for any of them.

Danny was the only one for whom returning to school was even an option. Since 1974 the Massachusetts public school system has been required by a law known as Chapter 766 to design alternative programs for students who cannot function in regular classrooms. Before 1974 schools effectively discouraged returning dropouts by the simple expedient of putting them back into the last grade they had attended. Even if Duane, Jack, Billy or Stan had wanted to continue their education (which none of them did), the prospect of returning to the sixth or seventh grade would have been enough to change their minds. For them the only alternative to the street was the unlikely possibility of getting a job and keeping it. They would present themselves to prospective employers as school dropouts with criminal records and no training. With three strikes already against them, they would have to be willing to work harder for less money and at more menial tasks than their more qualified competitors on the job market. "Staying straight" would mean sticking to some mind-numbing job, even while knowing a lot more money could be made hustling on the street. The boys had gotten into trouble because of their lack of self-discipline, maturity and integrity. Now, ironically, to get out of trouble they would have to display more of these same qualities than was common among even the most upright sixteen-year-olds.

At one time or another all of them had shown us glimpses of the kids they might have been had they been born into different worlds. But sixteen years of conditioning could not be undone in three months. They were still basically delinquents, for whom "going home" meant returning to the same environments that had led them to Penikese. Duane and Jack would be going back to families that had pretty much abandoned them to the street. Bill would once again become the black-sheep stepson to an aggressively successful stepfather. Stan would again be tempted to drown his depressions in alcohol, while Danny could look forward only to the uncertainty of yet another foster home.

They all knew this, and in moments of candor they admitted to the near certainty of "getting busted" again once back in their own communities. Consequently we assumed that they would jump at alternatives to going home if we could come up with good ones.

Woods Hole once again rose to the occasion. Duane was offered a job at the village boatyard and a place to live with a nearby family. Dan Clark bumped more qualified applicants to hire Jack and Bill to live and work with his construction crew on a job in Gloucester. Worth Campbell, a local minister, offered a home to Danny, and the Falmouth High School agreed to admit him to its alternative-education program. Pete, our private student, would be going off to boarding school. Only Stan would have none of these plans, his horizons extending no farther than to the prospect of getting us "off his case."

We were elated. Thanks to the generosity of many people, all but one of our first graduates were to get what appeared to be their very best possible chance for a decent future. Consequently we were all the more perplexed when the kids, who had been enthusiastic about these various plans when we had first proposed them, became visibly uneasy at the prospect of their becoming a reality. Duane was the first to crack.

He went home for Thanksgiving and failed to return with the rest of the kids the following Monday. I drove up to New Bedford that evening and found him at his home with his mother.

"Hey Duane, what's going on?" I demanded. "We held the boat two hours waiting for you. You might at least have called if you weren't coming back."

"I ain't goin' back to that fuckin' island. No way."

"Why not? I thought you liked it there. Besides, you left that damned pump engine in a million pieces. You're the only one who knows how to put it back together, so you've got to come back. OK?"

"I told you already, I ain't going back. You or anybody else tries to make me, I'm gonna make you wish you hadn't. Go ahead! Just try me!"

"Come on, Duane. We've got less than a month until we close down. The judge told you that all you've got to do is finish up with us and he'll drop your charges, remember? If you quit now, DYS will probably just send you somewhere else."

"Ain't nobody sendin' me anywhere!"

"Well, goddamnit, at least give me a reason! When we came in last Wednesday, you told me you didn't ever want to leave the island."

"I don't have to give you nothin', man."

"Fair enough!" I turned to Duane's mother. "What do you think he should do, Mrs. Soares?"

True to form, she began to waffle. "Oh, I just don't know. I'm so lonely here all alone, an' he don't listen to anything I say, an' I just don't know what I'm gonna do. Honest, I don't." She looked imploringly at her boy. "Why don't you go back with the man, honey? I'll be alright I guess."

Duane threw a nutty. "*Fuck You, Mom.*" he yelled. "That ain't what you been tellin' me before!" He kicked over a table, breaking a lamp, and ran out the door.

"Lord Jesus help me," said Mrs. Soares.

"Where do you think he'll go?" I asked her.

"Down the street to the body shop. The back door's not locked. That's where he always goes."

I followed Duane to the body shop.

"Get the fuck outta here," he yelled. "Why don't you just leave me alone?"

He was in such a state I was afraid he might hurt himself, so I sat down on a truck running board and waited. After a while his rage subsided into quiet sobbing, but he remained too upset to talk. "You hang in there, Duane," I said. "Things 'll work out for you, OK?"

"OK."

I left him there.

In court two days later he repeated his threat that he would run if DYS "sent him away" ever again. His caseworker, who previously had been adamantly opposed to his going back to live with his disturbed mother, backed down, and Duane returned to the street.

Jack stuck it out until graduation before losing his nerve. The day before he was supposed to go up to Gloucester he called to say he had decided to stay in Fall River.

"Jesus, Jack," I told him. "You know Fall River's a dead end for you."

"Yeah, George. I know it is," he said sadly and hung up.

Bill was pressured by his stepfather into going to work for Dan Clark in Gloucester but quit two weeks later. The day after he returned home, he was picked up for another armed robbery.

Saddest of all was poor, vulnerable Danny. Initially his colorless personality had made him a hard boy to like. Our feelings about him changed as we began to realize how desperately he hoped to find through Penikese the sense of belonging that he needed so badly. Initially the prospect of a home in Woods Hole made him happier than we had ever seen him. But Danny also faltered when faced with the possibility of having his dream come true. When asked by his caseworker whether he wanted to stay with us in Woods Hole or go back to the foster home he had stayed at unsuccessfully once before, he hung his head and said he didn't know. His caseworker, whose nose was out of joint because we hadn't adequately involved him in the plans to find Danny a home in Woods Hole, elected to send him back to the scene of his earlier unhappiness.

We finished 1973 with the realization that the job we had undertaken was not going to be what we expected. If our first students were in any way representative of the DYS boys we would be working with, most were going to be a whole lot different from the romanticized image of the "old-fashioned delinquents" I had from my days in the Marine Corps.

Looking back over the first three months, we decided our worst mistake in dealing with the kids was to underestimate how ingrained were the attitudes responsible for delinquency. In our original proposal to DYS we advocated the value of physically demanding outdoor activity as a means of building self-confidence in boys whose only means of proving their manliness to themselves and their peers were illegal. We still believed in the value of this approach, but we were beginning to see that our job had to go beyond simply bolstering self-confidence.

We had assumed boys would react favorably if given responsibility. We believed that if we demonstrated that we trusted them, they would respond by living up to our trust. Because we thought in terms of their futures, we assumed they recognized that what they did or failed to do now would have favorable or unfavorable consequences later. Instead we discovered that the kids who came to Penikese were raised to see the world in far different terms from our own. They thought no further than indulging the desire of the moment. The idea of incurring any immediate hardship for the sake of some future good made little sense to them. Responsibility was also a meaningless concept. Anyone dumb enough to trust them was fair game to be "ripped off." Their whole outlook was geared to beating the system. We were on the island to make them work, and their objective was to see how little work they could do without having us "get on their cases." They liked us individually, but they had no compunctions about stealing from us when they stayed with us. Nor did they have much group loyalty among themselves. They stole from each other just as they stole from us. They had no scruples against informing on one another if there was advantage to the informer in doing so. What was startling was the realization that they behaved this way without malice. They expected the same treatment from others. It was their way of life.

Nonethless we remained optimistic. We attributed the boys' collapse at the end of the year simply to lack of confidence. The attitudes they brought with them, which resurfaced when they left, reflected their accommodation to the world as they saw it. They had learned to live with being unwanted. They knew the ritual of failure at school. They had found companionship and even status in the subculture of delinquency. We were asking them to turn their backs on a way of life that, however unhappy, was at least familiar. By pushing them towards more conventional goals — a job, school, straight friends — we were asking them to rejoin a society that had already rejected them, to compete in a league where being street-tough counted for little and where their lack of education and social skills were major liabilities. No wonder each one lost his nerve.

"We believe," concluded our 1973 report, "that most delinquents would go straight if they thought they could make it in straight society. Our job is to teach them that they can." To do this we would need more time. Consequently we decided to scrap the six-week survival courses we had originally proposed to DYS and to reopen the following spring as a more long-term residential program aimed at teaching kids that they could in fact go straight.

Before we could reopen at all, however, we would have to find money enough to pay off our remaining bills from 1973 and to carry on for the eight to ten weeks we would need to operate in 1974 before we could expect our first check from the state. Our bank balance on the day the kids went home was $23. A day or so after Christmas, Herman and I sat down in our "executive offices" to ponder how to placate our growing list of creditors.

Herman thumbed through our mountainous stack of unopened bills. "Jesus, look at them. Wood Lumber Company. Hathaway for that damn winch. Here's another one from Falmouth Coal, they'll be shutting us off on boat fuel pretty quick if we don't pay that one. Can't have that."

He put Falmouth Coal aside and continued rifling through the stack. "MacDougalls' for the injectors. Charlbet's — that one'll keep another month. Gun & Tackle. Woods Hole Marine. Abbot and Dorothy Stevens . . . Abbot and Dorothy Stevens? What'd we buy from them?"

"Dunno. Let me see it." I looked at the envelope. "It says Abbot and Dorothy H. Stevens *Foundation*, you jerk. Open it, quick!"

Inside was a check for $10,000.

9

WEDNESDAY, APRIL 10, 1974, found me and three unenthusias-tic assistants building a fence around our vegetable garden on Penikese.

"Brad," I roared to the boy who a week earlier had been stealing cars in Brockton, "get away from that damn radio and dig that hole."

"Aw, fuck this shit," he yelled in return, hurling his shovel past the head of another boy and stomping off to the house.

What to do? Should I go haul the son of a bitch back out of the house, or should I profit by his absence and try to get something done on the fence? My other two assistants, veterans respectively of larceny and assault, bent self-consciously to their work, eyeing me furtively to see how I would react. I concluded that a show of force was more important than finishing the fence.

"Ken and Jeff, I'm going to get Brad. How about setting the three posts we've dug holes for? Line them up with the rest of the row and tamp the dirt in around them good and hard."

"Sure, no problem."

I went off to the house and found Brad carving his initials into the kitchen table. "Brad," I reasoned, "we've got to get that fence up to keep the rabbits out of the garden. They're already into the peas."

"Fuck the fence! Fuck the peas! Fuck the rabbits! I want off this fuckin' island. The whole place sucks. You suck!" he added, warm-ing to his subject.

"Well, that may be, but as long as you're here you are damn well going to work on that fence. Let's go."

"I won't."

"You will."

He did, thank God, as I wasn't sure what I was going to do next.

We returned to the garden to find Ken and Jeff leaning on their shovels. "Got 'em all in," they announced, nodding towards the three posts, which jutted off at crazy angles to the rest of the fence line.

Now what to do? The two kids seemed genuinely proud of their accomplishment. But how in Christ's name could anyone screw up so simple a job so completely? Perhaps this was a more subtle rebellion. Jeff, particularly, looked suspiciously smug. Nonetheless I figured I'd give them the benefit of the doubt. ·

"Not too bad," I remarked. "Brad, let's see if we can straighten the line up a bit. I'll sight along the other posts and you push the tops the way I tell you."

But Brad had gone back to the house. "Oh, goddamnit," I thought to myself, "what the hell am I doing here, anyhow?"

One week before, we had herded twelve unruly boys along with two goats onto *Nereis* and set off to begin our second season on Penikese. Among a pretty scruffy group, the most striking of our new students was tall, scraggly-haired, buck-toothed Jeff, who arrived wearing a top hat. His hat had blown overboard, and nothing had gone right since.

Our troubles were of our own making. So as not again to put our financial fate in the hands of our nemesis, Jack Haywood, the DYS Region VII assitant director, we opened enrollment to the other six regions. We didn't even insist on interviews as a condition to enrollment. Our announced policy was that "since Penikese provides kids the chance for a new start unencumbered by their previous reputations, we, like the Foreign Legion, will take anyone who volunteers."

The practical result of this naive altruism was to amass on one small island what was probably the most disturbed group of adolescents to be found anywhere in Massachusetts. Although all of the regions had seen in our open-admissions policy a heaven-sent opportunity to unload kids that other programs would not even consider, Region IV, with jurisdiction over Chelsea and Charlestown, led the league in the irresponsibility of the referrals it made to

Penikese. Among their first four "volunteers" to the island were two dangerously unstable psychopaths, one boy who was terrified of the water, and the president of Chelsea's most notorious street gang.

To look after this group of hellions we had a staff that, although larger than the preceding year's, was a good deal younger and less experienced. Chip Jackson had left to resume his artistic career. David, Herman and I made up the old guard. Our three new staff, Jack Simonds, Dickey Edwards and Ship Densmore, were all level-headed and competent, but they were so close in age to our students that at the start their claims to authority were tenuous at best.

The staff's job was made harder by the fact that the kids who arrived in 1974 were clearly marching to a different drummer than had their predecessors. During the push to get up the house the year before, the adults on Penikese, counting both staff and volunteers, often outnumbered the students and so set the tone. But now, with only two staff on island at any one time to supervise twelve kids, the students were playing for the approval of their peers, not their instructors. Status among delinquents came from being the "meanest motherfucker," and we had twelve contenders for that title.

"Fights," David noted, "have been almost daily, and at no time can we safely leave groups of boys alone."

Some boys couldn't even be safely left by themselves. Mark was a dim-witted Goliath from Springfield who was oafishly pleasant except during his fits of temper. He blew up one evening over some trivial matter and stomped away into the darkness. Rather than follow, the staff decided to let him cool off on his own and so thought no more about him until a commotion down at the pier attracted their attention.

Dickey Edwards ran down to the water too late to prevent Mark from taking off in our only skiff. The water was still too cold to swim in, so Dickey could only watch helplessly as Mark rowed out to *Nereis*, which he attempted to steal.

By the time Herman got word over the radio that all this was going on, Mark had abandoned his efforts to start the diesel, ripped out the ignition wires in frustrated rage, lost one of his oars, and was paddling off toward Cuttyhunk with the other one.

The current running between Penikese and Cuttyhunk is so strong that no one, no matter how powerful, can paddle across in a heavy skiff with only one oar. When Dickey lost sight of Mark, the ebb tide, with two hours still to run, was carrying him toward the open ocean. So Herman notified the Coast Guard while I roared off for Penikese as fast as our boat would carry me.

Halfway down along the islands I heard the Coast Guard helicopter passing overhead, while over the radio crackled traffic from the cutter *Point Jackson*. The two forty-one-footers from the Menemsha Coast Guard base on Martha's Vineyard were already on the scene. We searched all night in a freshening breeze and had about given up when the helicopter's powerful searchlight spotted our skiff ashore on the west end of Cuttyhunk. Someone had pulled the boat well up on the beach, and we hoped that someone was Mark.

Sure enough, later that morning Mark showed up on the town pier, well pleased with his adventure and ready to return to Penikese as if nothing had ever happened. "Aw, I'd 'ave made it," he boasted when we told him where he might have ended up if the current had not turned in time to carry him back in to shore.

Although he was really too retarded to realize the severity of what he had done, we had to throw Mark out, both because he had shown himself too impulsive to live safely in our accident-prone environment and, equally important, as an example to the other kids. Two years later I learned that he had killed a little girl. Another hour of ebb tide might have averted that tragedy.

Our troubles did not end with Mark. We had learned that the kids needed occasional breaks from island life, so we insisted as our one condition to admission in 1974 that the DYS regions make arrangements for their kids to go off island every third weekend. Some regions, however, cheerfully ignored this provision, with the result that David's, Herman's and my families often ended up with not entirely welcome house guests on weekends.

Once that summer I brought home an almost feral boy named Harvey on such short notice that Yara and I were unable to cancel a dinner invitation we had accepted for the same weekend. Not knowing what else to do, we decided to drop Harvey off at the movies on our way to dinner and pick him up on our way back. This we did, but not before he had spotted our very pretty teenage babysitter.

Yara and I excused ourselves from dinner in time to get back to the theater by the end of the movie. Harvey was not there. We waited, thinking he probably had gone down the street for a hamburger. Twenty minutes passed and still no Harvey, so we drove home, annoyed he had run away but relieved that at least we would have the rest of the weekend to ourselves.

As we pulled into the driveway, Yara caught a glimpse of someone bolting out the back door. "Probably some bashful boyfriend," I laughed as I went out back to bring in the dogs.

When I got back to the house I found Yara with our sobbing babysitter in her arms. Harvey, it seemed, had hitchhiked back from the theater right after we dropped him off. At first he was so awkwardly polite that the girl had taken pity on him. And so for two hours they talked of their very different lives. Harvey spoke with incoherent poignancy of a childhood brutal beyond anything the girl could relate to her own experience, while she, with her grace and poise, introduced him to a world as foreign to him as his was to her.

Those two hours were possibly the happiest Harvey had spent in his short life. With television-inspired images of how such moments should end, he had misinterpreted the girl's kindness and become too familiar. She pushed him away and he, in puzzled anger, reverted to type. Providentially, we arrived in time to prevent a rape.

This was a real crisis, and the girl was its heroine. Although badly shaken, she was more worried about Harvey than herself, and she begged us not to report him to the police. I was of two minds about that. We were by now familiar enough with DYS to have seen the casual attitude that agency took toward repeated crimes by its charges, and I now felt the same temptation to downplay the whole incident. The girl was not hurt. Harvey was probably already halfway back to Chelsea, and Penikese certainly did not need the kind of publicity that would follow if the newspapers picked up a police report. There were already rumblings enough in the community about the bad element we were bringing into town.

On the other hand Harvey had committed a serious crime. The girl's family might insist on pressing charges, in which case my failure to report immediately to the police would prove awkward. Another uncertainty was Harvey himself. What if instead of running for home he was still in town looking for another girl? We would be in one hell of a fix if an unreported fugitive from Penikese committed a second violent crime in the community.

Then I came to my senses. "Jesus!" I thought, "here I am thinking just like Ted Kennedy at Chappaquiddick." I was reaching for the telephone when I heard steps on the back porch. It was Harvey.

Until this point I had felt, to put it mildly, little sympathy for our would-be rapist. So when I saw this boy knocking timidly at the back door I did not know what to make of it. What the hell was he doing back here, anyhow? Harvey was no stranger to the street, so he certainly could have no fears about fending for himself on the run. He was also savvy enough to realize that he was turning himself in for a serious crime. Why had he come back?

I asked him. "Dunno," he mumbled. "Is she all right?" Then he broke down. "Shit," he wept. "She was so nice, an' now she ain't never gonna want to see me again. Everything I do, I fuck up. *Everything.*"

Poor bastard. I called the girl's mother, who very decently agreed with her daughter not to press charges. That at least solved the problem of the police, since with Harvey back and no charges pending, there was nothing to report. But our troubles were still far from over. Woods Hole was too small a town for a scandal like this one not to get around. I knew there would be gossip, and I felt at the very least we should show that Penikese would not continue to menace the community with a proven bad element. Harvey would have to go, and the sooner the better.

It was by now Sunday morning. After many phone calls I managed to track Harvey's caseworker down at his home. He was not happy to hear from me. "Look," I explained, "for Penikese and DYS to retain any credibility in this town, you've got to get this kid out of here fast. Don't you see that?"

"Yeah," he said, "but it's Sunday. I don't work weekends."

"Well, who does? There must be someone in your office on duty Sundays. Jesus! You're telling me DYS just closes up on weekends? What if he really had raped that girl? What would you do then?"

"Dunno. Call the police, I guess. Look, man, I'm sorry, but there's nothin' I can do. Call me tomorrow, OK?"

He hung up. Harvey and I went off overnight in my sailboat, and I turned him over to DYS the following day.

The next disaster that summer had all the ingredients of a Marx Brothers comedy. Rotating the staff on Penikese posed the same dilemma presented by that old riddle concerning the cannibals and the missionaries faced with crossing a river without allowing cannibals to outnumber missionaries on either bank. Occasionally our system collapsed as it did one Sunday, when in order to get people and boats all to the right places we had to leave Herman alone with the kids until David, who was going off duty, could get into Woods Hole in *Nereis* and I could run her back down to join Herman on the island.

David departed, and Herman immediately found himself confronted with the task of riding herd on the kids, no two of whom wanted to do the same thing. Some wanted to fish, some to sail, some to swim. The only activity that met with unanimous approval was to visit Cuttyhunk. Everyone promised to be very good. So Herman packed the whole crew into *Sagitta* and steamed across to the Cuttyhunk town pier, where his tour group promptly dispersed to the four winds leaving their leader to search in vain all afternoon for his charges.

Herman finally returned to Penikese to await reinforcements. Unsuspecting, I arrived later that evening; the two of us immediately raced over to Cuttyhunk. There to our horror we found a huge outdoor cocktail party of yachtsmen already in full swing on the end of the old Coast Guard pier. "Holy Mother!" said Herman, because even before we pulled alongside we could hear raucous hoots rising above the murmur of polite conversation and see unyachtsman-like figures weaving unsteadily among the crowd.

We rounded up these revelers as unobtrusively as possible and came up one short. Craig, our own Mr. Cool, was still in town where he had been seen earlier smoking pot in company with a summer girl.

I found the two of them easily enough. Getting Craig back to the boat was another matter. "I ain't comin'," he advised. "I'm gonna live with Cathy. She says it's OK with her mom, ain't it, Cathy?"

Cathy assured me that her mother was ready to welcome Craig into her family with open arms.

This was a new one. I tried reason. "For chrissake, Craig. You know you can't do that. Why don't you get Cathy's address, and you two can keep in touch, OK?"

"No way, man! I'm stayin'."

Cathy gazed at him with adoring eyes.

I thought of Herman struggling to hold those other eleven kids in *Nereis*—"like trying to keep frogs in a bucket" as he later described it—and I knew there was no more time for argument.

"Come on, Craig," I commanded. "We're going."

"Fuck you!"

So I dragged him away on my shoulder with Cathy following along behind shouting in a most unladylike way. There was no way this procession of ours was going to pass unnoticed through the cocktail party. Speed, therefore, seemed the only option. I plunged into the party, trying to force my way through to *Nereis* while Cathy and Craig made the welkin ring with shrieks and curses.

The horrified crowd parted before me. Herman had the lines off and the engine running. I was almost at the boat. A matron grabbed my arm.

"Here, you! What do you think you're doing? Put that boy down!"

"Oh, fuck off, Ma'am," I muttered and dove for the boat. I had been too long among delinquents.

10

D AVID WOKE UP one morning that same summer and found
most of our chickens flopping helplessly about on broken
legs. David, whom the kids called "Pops," and I never found out
for certain who was responsible for this atrocity. It was one of
the boys — that much is certain — since the seagulls, who were the
island's only natural predators, would not have broken so many
legs.

Besides, by midsummer 1974, our antennae had gotten pretty
good. We could sense from the kids' mood that they knew more
than they were telling. We could also see that most of them were
nearly sick at the sight of those dying birds flopping helplessly
about. But their revulsion at the deed did not match their fear
of the perpetrator ("He's gotta be psycho, right?"), so they kept
quiet.

There was only one chicken killer. If two boys had been involved
the truth would have eventually surfaced. Their secret would have
been twice as hard to keep, and the peculiar network of alliances
based on fear or friendship would have been twice as vulnerable
to collapse. One culprit quite possibly would have implicated the
other to avoid suspicion himself. Then there would have followed
a flurry of charges and counter-charges in the course of which the
two would invariably have tripped themselves.

Since I don't know for sure who did it, I can't tell the story
as it actually happened. What follows is, strictly speaking, fiction.
My recreation of the event is a composite, built from real incidents and real conversations. Its purpose here is to portray the way

many hard-core delinquents think and why they are so hard to reach.

Betcha didn't know you can break a chicken's leg an' he won't even squawk or nuthin'. I know. I done it with lots of 'em. Where I done it is in this program they sent me to after I got busted with Scott. Scott's my buddy. What happened is me an' him was hangin' down at the mall, an' this dude drives up in this bad fuckin' Camaro 327 with mag wheels an' the whole bit, man.

"Hey, check it out," I says to Scott, an' we check it out without even lettin' the dude know we're watchin' him. We sees him take his keys but the dumb fuck don't even bother to lock his doors.

"Check out where he's goin'," Scott says to me, so I follows him into the mall, an' I sees he's gettin' his hair styled, so I tells Scott we got plenty o' time, an' me an' him, we just kinda boogy on up to that Camaro like we owned the fuckin' thing. Scott's got his tools on him, an' he's got that car hot-wired so quick I don't know how he done it, an' we're outta there, but real slow like, 'cuz we don't want nobody noticin'. I mean, no patches or RDs or any shit like that. We go a couple o' miles, an' Scott pulls into this alley up behind this car that's parked there, an' we swap plates 'cuz we figure by now the dude's called the pigs. I jimmy the glove box an' find ten bucks an' a couple o' joints — so we pulls in fer Whoppers at the Burger King, an' after that we just kinda cruise around gettin' a buzz on from the joints an' checkin' out the chicks.

Trouble is, Scott ain't cool when he's been smokin', so pretty soon he's laughin' an hollerin', "Fuck you, bitch!" at the chicks an' swervin' all over the fuckin' road. I sees this red light up ahead, but Scott, he don't even try to stop, an' then there's this fuckin' blue light right behind us. Scott floors it, an' we runs a bunch more lights with sirens screamin' an horns blowin' an' fuckin' cars drivin' up on the sidewalks. By now my fuckin' heart's goin' faster'n that fuckin' Camaro, an' I'm hollerin' at Scott to stop fer chrissake before he gets both our asses killed, an' just then another cop car pulls out in front of us. Scott tries to turn, but he's goin' too fast an' he jumps the curb. I sees this broad carryin' groceries right in front of us. Her mouth is open like she's tryin' to scream, but she ain't makin' no sound an' then she goes under the fuckin' car with this kinda poppin' noise, an' bags an' carrots an' all that kind o' shit is flyin' all over the fuckin' place.

We hits this building an' go right through this big glass window, an' then we stop. For a minute nobody sez nuthin', an' then people start screamin'. Scott's got fuckin' blood all over his face. My ears is ringin' an' I'm tellin' myself I better book before the pigs get here, but while I'm thinkin' this about a million fuckin' squad cars pull up, an' that's how I got busted.

What happens then is that the broad with the groceries fuckin' croaks, an' Scott gets charged with homicide, an' now he's doin' hard time in Walpole, which is a bummer, man. I mean, he didn't mean to fuckin' hit her, ya know! It's her tough shit she got in his way.

Me? 'Cuz I'm only fifteen I'm still a juvenile, so I gets committed to DYS, which is cool 'cuz I already been committed two times, an' there ain't nuthin' they can do to you, an' when you're seventeen you get your record sealed so ain't nobody gonna know what you done, right? Anyways, I goes to court, an' this judge, he lays this line on me, but I can't understand what the fuck he's talkin' about except I know he's pissed. My caseworker from DYS is shakin' like he's scared shitless when he's talkin' to the judge, but when we gets outside the courtroom he tells me the judge don't have no business hasslin' me like he did, an' I don't have to sweat nuthin' 'cuz DYS an' not the judge is in charge o' me, an' DYS ain't into punishment like the judge is an' wants to help me with my problems. My caseworker, he's a cool dude. He's got an earring that's got a real diamond in it. No shit!

So I gets sent to Rozzie, which is where they lock us JDs up, but that's cool too, 'cuz lots of my friends is there, an' some o' the workers will sneak you grass if you got bread to pay for it. I'm there maybe two weeks when my caseworker comes to tell me he can get me into this program which is on an island where you can go fishin' an' waterski all day. I asks him how long I gotta stay there, an' he says if I plays it cool an' don't get in no more trouble he can get me home in two months. I don't want to go to no fuckin' program, but I can always split if I want to, an' also there's a couple o' black dudes on the third floor who is lookin' for me 'cuz I copped a joint from 'em, so I says to my caseworker that I'll check this Peckinese place out. Dumb fuckin' name, Peckinese. Lotsa programs got dumb fuckin' names. I was in *one once what was called Quest, an I asks the guy who runs it what the fuck does Quest mean, an' he says it means to try hard. Try hard! For what, fer chrissake? All's we done was sit around watchin' TV all day an' he calls that tryin' hard. Shit!*

Anyhow, where was I? Oh, yeah. I was tellin' you about the chickens. So I goes to this place Peckinese for a two-week trial, an' my caseworker an' me, we drives down to the Cape, an' before I gets on the boat which goes to the island this guy who's drivin' it feeds me this shit about bein' honest an' how the island is for kids who want to be there, which makes me want to laugh but I plays it real cool an' don't say nuthin'. We starts out, an' the fuckin' boat is bouncin' around in these giant fuckin' waves, an' they won't let me smoke even a butt. I am wishin' I stayed in Rozzie even with them black dudes lookin' fer me, but we finally gets to the island, an' I comes to find there ain't a fuckin' thing on it but these ratassed old houses they calls a fuckin' school. No TV, no electricity, no fuckin' nuthin'! Swear to God!

One thing they got plenty of is pigeons. This other kid who is there takes me around to see the island, an' these fuckin' pigeons is dive-bombing us everywhere we goes. I almost wings one with a stone, but this other kid says we ain't allowed to hurt the animals. He says they ain't pigeons either. They're seagulls. Pigeons, seagulls, who gives a shit? I finds this nest with babies in it, an' I waste the fuckers by stompin' on 'em. The other kid is mad I done it, but he's a wimp. I tells him if he says anythin' I'll break his fuckin' arm. An' can you believe it? When I'm tellin' him this the mother pigeon comes flyin' over an' shits right in my hair. Right in my fuckin' hair! I tells that other kid right then I'm gonna waste every fuckin' bird on that fuckin' island, an' I don't give a fuck who tries to stop me.

Then I sees the fuckin' boat is leavin'. Hey! I says, how do you get off this fuckin' place? The wimp says you don't, an' laughs. I asks him if they got pot here, an' he says not unless I brought it—which I did, but I don't tell this wimp I got any. He says the workers trust us not to bring pot from our weekends. Shit! I seen some dumb fucks since I been in DYS, but these guys that work at Peckinese are the worst. Trust us? I guess they ain't got the balls to shake us down.

Then this big dude they call Pops, who is the head worker, tells me I gotta stay there four months to graduate. Four fuckin' months on that fuckin' island! I tells Pops my caseworker says I only gotta stay two months, but he says it's four months, an' if I don't like it I can go off after my two-week trial. So where am I gonna go? Back to Rozzie an' get my ass kicked by them black motherfuckers? No way. I sees my caseworker an' this guy Pops an' all the rest of 'em has conned me into bein' stuck on this fuckin' rock an', believe me, I am some pissed! Hey, payback's a motherfuck, I says to myself, but with Pops I play it real cool.

Couple of days go by an' I'm bustin' my ass choppin' wood an' paintin' these boats they make there. I asks when're we goin' water-skiin', an I finds they ain't even got waterskis anywhere on the whole fuckin' island, so I knows they've conned me again but still I play it cool. Then Pops tells me I gotta wash dishes. Hey! I tells him, I ain't washin' no dishes. So he starts gettin' pissed, an' I tells him I didn't come to this fuckin' island to do no pussy work like washin' dishes. Anyhow I don't want no fuckin hassles, an' Pops is a big dude, so I starts in on them fuckin' dishes, an' I'm bangin' 'em around real loud just to show I don't take no crap off of nobody when this fuckin' bowl goes and breaks. Pops, he grabs my arm an' tells me to cool it, an' I tell him to get his fuckin hands offa me, an' I'm reachin' for this knife that's up behind the sink when he shoves me up against the ladder so's I hit my fuckin' head. Ain't nobody gonna pull that kinda shit on me — so I goes fer him, but this other dude that works there named Jack gets me in this hammerlock so I can't do nuthin'. Jack's one strong motherfucker.

After a while they lets me go, an' I goes up to the loft, which is where we sleeps, an' I pretends I'm sleepin'. For a while nobody is sayin' much downstairs, but then the other kids start screwin' around again an' laughin' an' I knows them pricks is laughin' at me. I hears somebody finishin' up them fuckin' dishes, who is probably Pops, an' I hears the rest of 'em playin' pool. The wimp is winnin,' an' I feel like goin' down an' whippin' his ass 'cuz there ain't nobody on that fuckin' island can beat me at pool except maybe Pops, but I don't want to even see any o' them pricks, so I stays where I am. One thing I gotta say about that fuckin' place is that they got real good food, an' the nighttimes is fun what with lanterns an' playin' pool an' all that kind o' shit.

The other kids starts comin' up to the loft an' makin' a fuckin' racket tellin' each other to shut up' cuz they think I'm sleepin'. Finally everybody is sleepin' except Pops who reads all fuckin' night in his rack. I gotta piss somethin' bad, but I ain't goin' to until he's sleepin', 'cuz I don't want no fuckin' speeches. I hears him turnin' about a hundred fuckin' pages, an' you better believe by then I am one hurtin' motherfucker. The prick.

Just when I can hardly hold on no longer I hears him blowin' out the lantern, an' start snorin'. They keeps a lantern lighted downstairs, so I can see where I'm goin' when I sneaks down the ladder without no shoes on or nuthin'. I ain't gonna make it to the stone posts which is where they tell us we gotta go to piss, so I runs out on the porch an' piss off the edge, which we ain't supposed to do, but I give a rat's ass. Soon as I'm done pissin' I find I gotta shit too, which is a bummer, 'cuz I gotta go all the way up to the fuckin' shithouse. I'm thinkin' maybe I'll shit in the cellar, but it's dark down there an' kinda scary so I goes up the hill to the shithouse with no fuckin' shoes or nuthin', like I says, an' freezin' my ass.

This shithouse they got is just a big hole in the ground with a house on top of it an' three seats where you sit an' shit in the hole. They even got a pink seat fer the broads, but I sits in the middle one where you can see out the window. The hole's so fuckin' deep when you let one go you gotta wait to hear it hit. Anyhow I'm sittin' there when suddenly this big fuckin' moon comes outta the water. First I'm thinkin' it's the sun, it's so fuckin' bright, but I knows it can't be no sun 'cuz it's night an' besides there's only half of it there. The whole fuckin' ocean is shinin' like it's silver, which makes me think about my mom who is always cryin' an' shit to make me feel bad. Then I starts thinkin' about my fuckin' dad beatin' on me just 'cuz I don't do good in school when he ain't even got no fuckin' job, an' I thinks about that prick, Pops, who won't let me piss when I gotta, an' my fuckin' caseworker who conned me onto this fuckin' rock, an' all the time I'm gettin' more an' more pissed.

I'm gettin' this funny feelin' like I'm high an' like I gotta do somethin' or else I'm gonna throw a nutty when I looks outta the window, an' I sees these fuckin' chickens sleepin' on top o' the fence all in a line, like. So then I remembers that fuckin' bird what shit on my head, an' I freaks out. I runs outside without wipin' my ass or nuthin'. Then I starts movin' real quiet like — like I was doin' a B an' E. I sneaks down behind that fence with the chickens on it, and I'm thinkin' o' what Pops told me that if you turns a chicken upside down it gets sorta' hypnotized an' don't do nuthin'. By now some o' them chickens is makin' noises like they is scared 'cuz they hear me, but they're too fuckin' dumb to fly away. Everything is still lookin' silver from the moon, an' I can even see the feathers on their tails all lined up 'cuz it's so fuckin' bright, an' they're all facin' the other way.

Pops is right. I grabs one o' them off the fence, an' he lets out a squawk, but I flips him ass end up real quick, an' after that he don't say nuthin'. So there I am holdin' onto this fuckin' chicken without knowin' what I'm gonna do next when I sees him lookin' up at me real quiet like, an' I don't know why then but instead o' seein' that chicken I find I'm lookin' at that broad with the bags just before she goes under the car. I sees her eyes, an' I'm thinkin' of Scott up there in Walpole gettin' buttfucked by them fuckin' lifers an' I knows that's where I'm goin' too, an' all the time I'm gettin' more pissed but scared too, an' then that fuckin' chicken starts squirmin' in my hands.

So now I'm really freaked. It's colder 'n hell, but I'm sweatin' an' hangin' onto that fuckin' chicken 'cuz I knows if I puts him down he's gonna squawk an' maybe wake up Pops. Then somethin' weird happens. Suddenly I don't feel nuthin' at all. I grabs that chicken I'm holdin' by his leg an' twists 'til I feel it pop just like I'm breakin' drumsticks at Kentucky Fried Chicken. I breaks his other leg an' throws him down, thinkin' that'll teach the fucker not to shit in my hair.

He don't squawk or nuthin' but just kinda drags away with his wings hangin out an', can you believe it, them other chickens is still all sittin' up there on the fence. So I goes right down the line, breakin' their fuckin' legs — pop, pop, pop, just like that — an' none of 'em say nuthin', just like I said before. After that I'm real tired, so I goes back to bed.

Next morning after Pops wakes us up I comes down and find that Molly, who's one of the broads what works there, is actin' real upset. "Whatsa matter?" I asks her, an' she tells me somethin's happened to the chickens. Jeez! I'd already forgot all about them fuckin' chickens. Anyways, all the kids come runnin' down, an' we goes up to the chicken pen to see whatsa matter, an' there's fuckin' chickens lyin' all over

the fuckin' place. When they sees us comin' some of 'em start flap-
pin' an' draggin' their asses around the ground, but most of 'em just
lie there. They got this kinda ramp what goes up to the chicken house
an' one of 'em tries to get up the ramp, but he can't make it an' keeps
fallin' off, which is comical an' I starts to laugh but nobody else is
laughin', so I stops when I sees that wimp kid lookin' at me funny.

That day nobody says much, an' everbody's walkin' around like
somebody had fuckin' died or somethin'. I mean, what the fuck, man?
They're just a bunch o' fuckin' chickens, so why is everybody makin'
such a big deal about it? Pops, he sends us all back to the house, an'
he kills all the chickens what has got broken legs. All the kids is whis-
perin' back an' forth about who done it, an' I lets on that it was the
wimp an' he starts to fuckin' cry. Can you believe it? What a fuckin'
pussy!

When Friday comes we all got weekend passes, an' the boat takes
us back to Woods Hole which I thought was the fuckin' sticks when
I first seen it but after bein' on that fuckin' rock now it looks like
fuckin' civilization with cars an' all that kinda' shit. My caseworker
is waitin' for me, an' him an' Pops, they talk real serious like, which
I knows is about me an' then they tells me that I flunked my fuckin'
trial an' can't go back to the island. I am some pissed! That fuckin'
Pops an' the rest of 'em, they screwed me good. Shit! It was Pops an'
not me what killed those fuckin' chickens, an' they don't even know
it was me that done it, an still they make me go back to Rozzie where
them black dudes is waitin' for me. Fuckers! Oh well, like I was sayin',
payback's a motherfuck. I'll be lookin' for those fuckers on Peckinese.

11

___

A S THE SUMMER OF '74 wore on and we gained in experience, disasters became fewer. The island was again working its magic. Salt air, plenty of exercise and freedom from the unremitting tension of street life all combined to work a calming influence on hyper kids. Another calming influence was the arrival of women on Penikese. In July a self-confident girl named Molly Meigs began work as a volunteer and quickly made us realize our error in having previously ruled out women staff. We thought that insecure boys confronted with new challenges would be less self-conscious in an all-male environment. As it turned out the kids felt in many ways less threatened by Molly than by the rest of us. Evidently they felt there was less risk in dropping their guards around a woman.

Molly had just graduated from college with a degree in drama and soon had us all involved in impromptu skits in which the kids would play the parts of their parents, the victims of their crimes, court officials and policemen. Our actors were much more open in the roles they played than they dared be in real life. Beneath their slapstick comedy lay barely concealed pictures that were sad and startling. Uncaring parents, doltish bureaucrats and brutal police paraded across our stage against a backdrop of constant violence.

Caroline Smith, a beautiful girl who had worked as a welder for General Dynamics, joined Molly on the staff later that summer, and shortly afterwards our female contingent was doubled with the arrival of two graduate-student "duck ladies" who took up residence on the island to run an experimental effort to transplant nesting colonies of eider ducks to Massachusetts. As a result of this influx,

Penikese became a much happier place—which is not to say that all was roses for the women who worked on the island. Not many of our kids had any inhibitions about hitting a girl, and fewer still had reservations about using the crudest kind of abusive language in their presence. On top of all that, Molly and her successors had to deal with all the normal adolescent male hangups along with some that were not so normal.

We found out quick enough that street kids carry around some pretty bizarre attitudes about women. Although mothers are usually the strongest adult figures in their lives, the relationship between mothers and their delinquent sons seems more often than not to be fueled by guilt. "Oh, Johnny," asks the delinquent's mother in word or action, "why do you make me suffer so?"

Johnny cannot answer. In his shamed confusion over his compulsion to hurt the only person who loves him, he is driven to lash out against her again. More guilt leads to more resentment against the person who makes him feel guilty, and so the cycle repeats itself until in some strange way a mutual dependence on inflicting pain on each other becomes the bond between mother and son. Many kids project this basic emotional experience onto the world at large, so that inflicting pain becomes their only means of relating to others.

Mothers, in any event, are a separate category. All other women are either "skags" or "foxes." "Skags" are ugly. "Foxes" are not. The role of the fox is to bat her eyes at manly posturing. During that summer it came as a revelation to our students to meet four very pretty women who were not only individuals in their own right but who could also hold their own at pushups.

Around Thanksgiving the kids began their countdown towards going home. Tension rose. Street talk and street mannerisms that had been put away for the summer were brought back out again and dusted off. Jeff, of the top hat, who for the first time in his life found himself popular with his peers, succumbed to end-of-the-year pressure and stole Yara's car while on a weekend with us in Woods Hole. Since he usually spent most of his days off in bed, we had not noticed his absence until he called us from Fall River to report indignantly that the car was out of gas and to demand that we come pick him up.

"Pick you up?" I asked in amazement. "You steal our goddamn car, and now I'm supposed to pick you up?"

"Hey, I didn't steal it, man. That's why I'm callin' you up. If I'da stealed it, I wouldn't be callin' you up tellin' you where I'm at. Right?"

"Oh, horseshit! So, you didn't steal it. What did you do?"

"Dunno, just went for a ride, I guess. Now, you gonna pick me up, or what? I mean it ain't my fault it ran outta gas. I was gonna bring it back if it hadn'ta run outta gas."

How could you argue with logic like that? I picked him up.

Duane, Danny and Jack had acted much the same way at this same time the year before. Like those three, Jeff had also found on Penikese a sanctuary that he now was being forced to leave. The same eccentricities that from his earliest memories had made him and his family oddballs in their hometown had suddenly become assets to him on the island. His quick wit and quirky collection of trivial facts made him popular with the staff, and the fact that we liked him led the other kids to look at him in a different light as well. A popular recreation became watching Jeff take on the staff in good-natured verbal duels.

"Hey, David!" he announced one night at dinner. "Betcha didn't know watermelons is eighty-five-percent made of water."

"You're wrong," said David. "Watermelons are ninety-three-percent water."

Jeff pondered his reply while the other kids waited to see if their champion was to be outdone. "Fuckin' inflation!" he announced. "They've gone up!"

Everyone laughed, not at Jeff but at his joke, and he was so proud he almost burst.

Penikese also gave him the chance to show off his skill at cabinet-work. He could build things himself, and he had tact enough to help his less-talented friends without lording his superior skill over them, as under different circumstances they certainly would have done to him. So it was that the same boys who at home would have been among his tormentors began coming to him for advice on their shop projects.

Jeff had also found a niche for himself on his weekends, which he spent alternately at Herman's house and mine, and I think it meant something to him to be even temporarily part of two reasonably together families.

All of this was confusing to someone who had accepted society's verdict that he was a loser. Jeff was another boy who, although not happy with the accommodation he had made to the world, was at least at home in his role of weirdo. Penikese had raised the possibility in his mind that this role was not inevitable. Jeff knew how to be weird. He was less confident he could handle popularity and success. Faced with the prospect of going home, he lost his nerve. I think it was no accident he chose to steal our car. He was close enough to my family to need to prove to us, as well as to himself, that our hopes for him were misplaced. Being Jeff, he put his own peculiar twist on things by calling up afterwards to make sure we got the point. Most people fear failure. Jeff feared success.

It took us a while to recognize how much insecurity lay hidden beneath arrogant exteriors. With the wisdom of hindsight I came to see I had made a mistake by cornering Brad that day when we were working on the garden fence. My ultimatum that he get back to work put him in a position where he could not do what I demanded without losing face, and face was about all he had.

Brad was walking proof of the maxim that the importance of saving face increases proportionately with the degree of an individual's insecurity. Like his friends who burned lighted cigarettes between clenched forearms or who jumped sixty feet into the Quincy quarries, he was driven to such apparent daring by the even greater fear that to refuse would brand him as a "pussy." Most delinquents are too insecure to turn down a dare, and I had that day dared Brad to disobey me.

If there had been other kids present he probably would not have been able to back down. As it was he capitulated to superior force, but the only effect of my small victory was to further humiliate an already beaten boy. I had done little more than confirm what his childhood had already taught him. Might makes right. The meanest motherfucker rules the roost.

Seventy years earlier, Dr. Parker had run into similar conflicts with his patients at the leprosarium on Penikese. "It is incumbent on the management," he wrote in 1907, "to pursue a course of tact and goodwill, with relative laxity of discipline in unimportant matters while holding the inmates to rigid obedience and regularity in essentials." Tact and goodwill might be a bit hard to summon up when being called an asshole by some adolescent, but nonetheless the doctor's policy applied equally to our staff. The trick we were learning was always in any confrontation to leave a boy with a way out.

Every day at Penikese there were countless battles of will between staff and students. The staff member would want something done, and the kid's instinct would be to refuse to do it. If the staff member played his cards wrong the two of them would end up like two dogs, head to head, neither really wanting a fight, but neither knowing how to extricate himself with honor.

Our job was not to let matters reach that point. The kids could be counted on to blunder into confrontations. But once they had wised off or dug their heels in, they were as uncomfortable with the escalating tension as we were. The difference was that they did not know how to defuse the situation they had created without risking the humiliation of publicly backing down.

"Hey, John! It's your turn for dishes."

"Ain't doin' no dishes, man. Washin' dishes is pussy work."

"Oh? Who did them yesterday?"

"Peter done 'em."

"So Peter's a pussy? Is that what you're saying?"

"Nah! Peter's cool. He ain't no pussy."

"Well, you aren't, either. Now hurry up and get those dishes done so we can play that game of chess you said you could beat me at."

"So you rinse for me, an' I'll play chess wit' you. OK?"

"Jesus Christ! OK, you wash, I'll rinse."

Variations on this type of exchange, repeated dozens of times daily, can be wearing. Getting up and outside for exercises in the morning, making beds and sweeping down, cooking and washing up, assigning everyone to "doing school" or to various work projects, even getting them involved in volleyball or basketball at the end of the working day, all had the potential for tension. Over the years our most effective staff members have been those who have had the intuition to sense trouble coming and the "tact and goodwill" to head it off without compromising on Dr. Parker's "essentials."

But on Penikese, as everywhere else, the threat of force remains the alternative of last resort. My mistake with Brad had been to play what should have been my last card first.

Another attitude we mistakenly attributed to arrogance was the kids' know-it-all cockiness. To hear them talk they had the world by the tail. At sixteen they had "already had plenty o' jobs," and they could get another one any time they wanted. They "didn't need no more school." They knew all about carpentry. They were experts at engines. Their criminal records were no problem. "What the fuck, man? When you're seventeen they seal your record, right? So who's gonna know?"

At the root of all this bombast was once again the desperate need to save face. For all their boasting, our gang knew they were losers. What they wanted more than anything else was to be like "regular kids." Even our most successful delinquent, Richie, the president of Car Thieves of America, confessed in a rare moment of candor that he would go straight if he thought he could make it.

"But why couldn't you make it?" I asked him. "You're a good athlete. You've only been here a week, and already you've got the rest of the gang following you around like sheep. Christ, Richie! You're the kind of natural leader I always looked for in the Marine Corps. Why can't you make it?"

"Dunno, man. Because I'm a fuck-up, that's why. Now get off my case, OK?"

Richie ran on his first weekend at home, and six months later he was shot dead in Chelsea. We never got to know him well enough to learn why he held himself in such low esteem. Whatever his reasons, he was as belligerently defensive about not knowing "what regular kids know" as were all our other delinquents.

They lacked information that we began by assuming was common knowledge to kids half their ages: the days of the week, how to count, how to make change, reading street signs, basic hygiene, biology ("Hey, Pops! Do rabbits lay eggs?"), geography ("You was in 'Nam? That's where niggers come from, right?"), and so forth. We found that the more formal our efforts at instruction, the more the gang would react to us as they had learned to react in regular classrooms. Wising off, disruptions, and great shows of not paying attention were all for the purpose of hiding from themselves and everyone else their fear that they could not "do school." Once we finally recognized this, we got pretty good at sneaking in teaching as part of other activities. Using a tape measure in the shop led naturally to fractions. Doubling recipes from the cookbook introduced proportions. Instruction manuals became reading texts, and the island itself provided a natural-history laboratory. The kids were easily discouraged, but basically they wanted to learn. The trick was never to publicly embarrass them. For a delinquent the next worst thing to being a pussy was to look stupid.

We also learned not to be upset by incompetence so monumental it almost approached an art form. Although the limited manual skills of our first students had dissuaded me from the boat-building scheme we had originally submitted to DYS, I still believed strongly enough in the therapeutic value of building things not to want to abandon the idea entirely. Consequently, before we reopened in 1974, Jack Simonds and I cut out the parts for a prefabricated bunk-locker combination of our own design. Our creation was not much to look at, but as Jack put it, "even an idiot could put it together." The idea was that the kids would build their own accommodations in the loft, and we looked forward to seeing how much imagination they would bring to this project.

A few kids, Jeff among them, did "get into" the job and turned out creditable results. The others, despite our efforts to help, did such poor work that Jack was led to wonder if they were not "fucking up on purpose." He was partly right. Although our blunderers were not consciously trying to ruin the job, their experiences since childhood had beaten out of them any incentive to even try to do well. They had failed so often in so many different ways they now found it less threatening to make no effort and accept the consequences than to try hard and risk failure once again. We found ourselves as a result of this unconscious defeatism constantly walking a tightrope between insisting on standards of performance high enough to be at least marginally acceptable in the real world and setting standards so high that kids would be discouraged into passive rebellion.

Although we learned a lot in 1974 about working with the kids DYS sent us, we made little headway with a problem that still baffles us: admissions. We realized our open-admissions policy was a failure. We also learned not to expect complete candor from DYS caseworkers trying desperately to place their more unruly charges. But we were unable to develop any workable criteria about whom to accept and whom to reject. Arsonists were out due to the fire hazards on Penikese. So were child molesters, since David and I often brought our own small children to the island. Other than those two prohibitions, our only caveat was a rather vaguely worded injunction against taking kids too impulsive or with too limited an attention span to function safely around knives, saws, open fires and other potential dangers.

The problem was that we were not able to discern a pattern between prior records and performance on the island. Those prior records were imperfectly documented in the reams of often illegible photocopied material that accompanied DYS referrals to the school. Court records, "psychologicals" and reports from other programs a candidate had attended all combined to present a picture that often did not square with the boy we later got to know on the island. Jeff had been described as "dull normal."

Interviews could be as misleading as written records. The sullen kids brought by their caseworkers to meet us in Woods Hole were not likely to open up enough to give us much idea of the person we were going to be living with for the next four months on the island. "Yeah, maybe I'll check it out" was their usual reaction, particularly if Penikese was the shortest of the various programs DYS offered them.

Our stock rejoinder to this was, "OK, but remember we're going to check you out too. If we think you're just 'doing time' on the island, we'll send you back to DYS and give your slot to someone else who really wants to get something out of being there."

"Yeah, man," our new recruit would reply. "That's cool."

As a guide to admissions, we developed a profile of our more successful students and came up with no conclusions that defied common sense. In general the less violent a boy's crimes, the more intact his family, and the further he had gone in school, the better he was likely to do on Penikese. For all practical purposes the only result of our profile was to identify the kind of boy DYS was least likely to send us. There was, however, one small surprise. We found no correlation between how a boy had done in prior programs and how he was likely to do with us.

Our problem was that many in DYS equated our island location with Alcatraz and saw Penikese as the ideal place to unload their time servers. Occasionally, however, we would be sent a kid who was either scared enough or realistic enough about the path he was on to want to change. Our job then was to give him confidence enough to try and the skills he needed to compete in straight society. Most of the time, however, we got kids who had too big a stake in their delinquent image to risk giving it up. We couldn't help them, because they didn't want help.

That distinction between boys who wanted to change and those still infatuated with the glamour of crime would have provided a good guide to admissions, if there had been any way of telling which was which. In reality, there wasn't. We could look forward to drawing both types to Penikese.

Knowing that, I wondered if it was not self-defeating to mix the two together. "Whoever has studied the interior of prisons and the moral state of their inmates," wrote de Tocqueville, "has become convinced that communication between these persons renders their moral reformation impossible, and becomes even for them the inevitable cause of an alarming corruption." Would the same be true of Penikese? Pete, who came closest to conforming to our profile for success, was as mortified as Danny had been the year before by his modest criminal record and lack of credible war stories. He went home determined to be as bad as his friends from the Island.

Two years later he was doing hard time.

12

"**A** HUNNERT!" came the cry from the cellar. "Hunnert an' fuckin' ten! — Twenty! *Whoee.* This mother's gettin' hot!"

We had built a sauna, and the kids loved it. In the evenings after dinner one of them would go down to stoke up the stove, and the rest would wait impatiently until our cedar-paneled hotbox came up to temperature.

Then the gang would compete to see who could stay longest on the highest bench. When one of them could stand it no longer he would rush naked and steaming into the cool night air, hollering "Water! Water!" until the assigned bucket man on the porch above doused him with cold water. After that our steam-cleaned citizen usually went promptly off to bed, which was why the staff was easily persuaded to allow saunas nearly every night.

Our second year was ending on the island, and we were getting pretty civilized. The main house, with its already smoke blackened beams and its walls festooned with lobster buoys, had acquired a very lived-in look. We had built a two-story barn and a second small dormitory known as Jack's House, both almost entirely from salvaged lumber. Our new sleeping quarters was, unfortunately, situated too close to the well. Piddlers, too scared or too lazy to make nighttime walks to the outhouse, began contaminating our water supply, so Jack's House became the School House, and its occupants were moved back to the loft.

Although we still had to haul water up from the well, we now had a salvaged stainless-steel sink which drained into a dry well dug in the garden. Our shower was a holed wooden bucket hung from the porch, and our refrigerator was an ancient propane model from a long-extinct manufacturer. All in all our standard of living was way up from the preceding year's.

We also upgraded our fleet. Two years of plugging back and forth from Penikese in *Nereis* had made us so yearn for speed that, somewhat against my better judgment, we bought what the Cutty-hunkers call a "whizzer boat" which we named after Dr. Parker but ended up calling the Blue Bomb. This twenty-three-foot open run-about was of a design derived from the offshore racing power boats and could get us from Woods Hole to the island in less than thirty minutes if it didn't break down, which it frequently did. The long hours I spent laboring over *Dr. Parker*'s engine, however, were small price to pay for meeting Leo Cohen, who owned the dealership where we bought the Blue Bomb.

Leo was a man of great and ever-changing enthusiasms. The first thing he did for the school was to organize his high-rolling colleagues into a group who called themselves the Friends of Penikese. The Friends were business people who had worked hard for their money and enjoyed spending it. They sponsored all kinds of benefits for the school, including a destruction derby at the local junkyard and an auction that was one of the high points of the 1974 Falmouth social season.

Like most auctions of donated items, this one offered a lot of good stuff along with a fair amount of junk. Bidding was high spirited, and often involved battles between business rivals who were less interested in the item on the block than in beating out the competition. What must unquestionably be the most expensive boat hook ever sold owes its place in history to one such rivalry. The auctioneer saw such little promise in this battered piece of hardware that he laughingly sold it to the first bidder for $1. At this a rather sodden member of the audience leapt angrily to his feet to protest that he had not been given the chance to bid. Hoots and jeers from the crowd only made this man more insistent until finally the original buyer offered to put his purchase back on the block. Leo then began the bidding at $100. The wronged man upped it to $125, and the crowd saw that they had him. Frenzied bidding followed, with the unfortunate and increasingly furious fellow doggedly topping every offer made. That boat hook finally sold for over $1,000.

All the improvements we made to our fleet and physical plant unfortunately were not enough to satisfy a new state agency known as the Office for Children (OFC). OFC had been launched with a lot of rhetoric concerning the Commonwealth's commitment to guaranteeing every child's right to "a fair and full opportunity to reach his/her full potential." In fact OFC's purpose was to establish standards for the state's already scandal-ridden network of private human-service contractors. This mission put OFC's new staff between a rock and a hard place. Established agencies such as DYS resented being relieved of the responsibility for evaluating their own contractors, while the contractors themselves objected to having to deal with yet another inflexible bureaucracy. These difficulties were compounded by the holier-than-thou attitude adopted by OFC's "child advocates" and by the fact that the office had no money of its own to subsidize the expensive upgrading it demanded of already-strapped private agencies.

The OFC licensing specialist who presented himself on Penikese came armed with a huge volume of regulations that plainly had not been written with an operation such as ours in mind. We were cited for our lack of running water, inadequate fireproofing, primitive kitchen facilities, absence of electricity, failure to install central heating, and the "number of flies allowed to enter the facility." Our staff was inadequately trained. We lacked professional therapists, and we offered no "counseling or therapy in the traditional sense."

Neither our inspector nor his supervisors at OFC were much moved by our contention that the therapy we offered on Penikese owed its effectiveness to the absence of the amenities OFC would have us install. We reiterated without success our belief in the value of an environment which promoted self-reliance and which was far enough removed from what our kids had known before to allow them to make a new start.

"You may be right," advised our licensing specialist, "but my hands are tied. Regulations are regulations, and I can't give you a license unless you comply with them."

"But how," we asked, "could we possibly comply with your regulations, even if we wanted to?"

"Beats me," he replied sympathetically, and climbed back on the boat.

Even more grating was OFC's contention that we lacked "professionalism." I got my back up over that one. "Goddamnit," I harumphed. "I spent ten years as an infantry officer. Herman has twice that much time driving merchant ships, and David's been knocking around with some pretty rough characters on the fishing boats. Aren't those experiences relevant to working with delinquents?"

"No," said the licensing specialist. "None of those experiences qualify you to provide the range of social, psychological and psychiatric services called for in the regulations."

"So tell DYS not to send us kids who need those services, for chrissake! Isn't this community-based experiment supposed to be creating a range of different programs for kids with different problems? Surely there's got to be fifteen or so Huck Finn–type delinquents somewhere out there who don't need shrinks. Send us those!"

The OFC man rolled his eyes. "Look," he said soothingly. "It says right here in paragraph three-point-oh-four, section six, subsection C of the Regulations for Licensure—"

"Licensure?" interrupted David, our grammarian. "There's no such word as 'licensure'. Don't you mean 'licensing?' I mean, we may not be professionals and all that, but we can speak English. That's helpful, don't you think, speaking English to the kids?"

"Hear, hear!" said Herman in his best professorial voice. "Perhaps among your regulations there should be one banning psychobabble and bureaucratese. Something like, say, "The licensee shall implement a plan whereby the chief administrative officer or his or her designee shall in accordance with the provisions of paragraph four-point-oh-one, section C, subsection three report to the Office incidents of neglect or abuse of the English language."

"Hey!" yelled the licensing specialist. "You guys want to get wise? You can take your goddamn island and shove it up your ass! Licensure. Licensing. Whatever it is, you keep up this shit and you ain't getting one. OK?"

"Good for you," laughed David. "No bureaucratese there."

We parted friends, although no closer to agreement. This impasse with OFC continued through the winter. March 1, 1975, the date we had intended to reopen, came and went with no solution in sight. By way of compromise OFC proposed that we limit enrollment to older boys, thus removing ourselves from their jurisdiction, since a child by their definition was any person under the age of sixteen.

No, we said, OFC should change, not us. We refused to withdraw our application for a license on grounds that Penikese should be a test case for the contention that the existing regulations were too inflexible to allow the wide spectrum of programs envisioned by the community-based experiment. Our motive for this stand was only partially one of principle. A more practical consideration was the fact that restricting ourselves to kids over sixteen would narrow our pool of applicants to only the saltiest, most difficult delinquents.

Mutual opposition to OFC was one of the rare issues that put Penikese and DYS on the same side of the fence. Its own policies having bankrupted a good number of its contractors, DYS now found OFC shutting down many of the rest. Fewer available "beds" for delinquents so increased public outrage at the department's inability to get bad kids off the street that pressure from high places was put on OFC to back off.

Late that April OFC conceded the inapplicability of its regulations to wilderness-based programs, and Penikese was allowed to reopen. Our first project for 1975 was to bring water into the main house. Jack Simonds and his carpenters set about roofing over the best of the three cisterns, while the rest of the gang, whom we christened "moles," began digging a three-foot deep, three-hundred-yard-long trench from the cistern to the house through ground that was more stone than soil.

Each huge rock we ran into acquired a personality of its own as the kids pondered the engineering problem it presented. One kid in particular, Fat Jack, usually advocated capitulation.

"We ain't never gonna move that rock, man. Fuckin' thing's been there a zillion years, an' you guys think you're gonna move it? Go 'round it, fer chrissake."

"No way!" said Roy. "That sucker's commin' outta there."

"Yeah? Show me," snorted Fat Jack, flopping languidly down to watch. Roy and his fellow activists rose to the challenge. Dirt and curses flew fast and furious. Sweat poured down bare, muddy backs, and quitting time went by unnoticed. Fat Jack grew cocky, "You guys should'a listened."

"Shaddup, you lazy sackashit. See, it's movin'!"

Pry bars were brought to bear. Slowly the rock rose from its home of a zillion years to roll clear of the trench.

"Still say it'a been quicker to go 'round it," Fat Jack resignedly opined as the cheering victors hustled him down to the water and tossed him in.

When the job was finally done, Roy, our Master Mole, was given the honor of opening the faucet, and a great cheer went up as a jet of muddy water splashed into the sink. After two years of hauling buckets up from the well the introduction of running water seemed the very height of luxury.

We had experimented unsuccessfully in 1974 with an arrangement that allowed kids to earn, through a combination of effort and longevity in the program, "shares" in the profits generated from the sale of garden produce and driftwood furniture. This complex scheme, intended to demonstrate the virtues of cooperative effort, instead caused nothing but resentment. Our more competent craftsmen, who produced the majority of the co-op's income, bitched about having to share equally with their less-talented colleagues and rebelled outright at supporting our "welfare cases" who contributed nothing.

To replace our failed co-op we began hiring our moles and carpenters at a maximum salary of $2 per day and paying them whatever percentage of this amount their instructors felt their conduct and performance warranted. Conduct was evaluated in terms of getting up on time, maturity, cooperation and honesty. Performance was rated by levels of effort, initiative, skill and care. Each of these eight categories was worth a maximum of 25 cents. This base pay could be supplemented by bonuses or reduced by fines. The point was to tie earnings to effort and, although the amount of money was not large, mighty labors were accomplished for the purpose of raising a score from $1.75 to $2.00.

Our third year, 1975, also saw the introduction of a more formal remedial-education program on the island. A graduate student, Jay Tashiro, interrupted his doctoral studies to join our staff that year. Jay used a remarkable combination of gentle humor and iron will to remotivate our cynical dropouts toward formal study. Undismayed by the boys' low tolerance to frustration and short attention spans, he produced impressive results, not the least of which was an almost 100-percent level of participation in an entirely voluntary program. "It's sad," he wrote in his end-of-the-year report, "to measure a sixteen-year-old boy's educational progress by his ability to recognize and write the months of the year. Yet this measure on a relative basis is a terribly important start."

Summer turned to fall and fall to winter. We had a good group of kids on the island, plenty of heat from the sauna, and the financial backing of Leo Cohen's friends. There seemed to be no reason to shut down. Two years of experience had demonstrated the disadvantages of interrupted operations. Running the school year-around would provide full-time work for the staff and eliminate the trauma of starting up cold each spring. We decided to do it.

"In November," David wrote in his log, "we planted winter rye in the garden, filled our huge compost bin with manure, seaweed and earth, and began preparing ourselves and our living quarters for our first winter on Penikese. On Thanksgiving Day a snowy owl arrived to spend the winter with us. In December the first snow fell, the winds increased, and the boat trips became unpredictable. Cutting driftwood gathered off the beaches into firewood took up more and more time. There was a stronger feeling of group pride, a spirit of 'us against the elements.' The feeling of the end of something, so evident at this time last year, was replaced by a more secure feeling of continuity."

1975 was a good year for us but a disastrous one for DYS. A series of well-publicized crimes by juveniles and escapes from DYS "intensive-care facilities" led to growing criticism of the department in the legislature and led ultimately to the resignation of Commissioner James Leavey. Leavey took the easy way out by blaming his problems on inadequate funding. In fact he had been hamstrung by the policies he inherited from his predecessor, Jerome Miller.

DYS in 1975 provided a case study on the pitfalls of idealism untempered by common sense. Miller's contention that a delinquent should have a say in his own rehabilitation had led to a system which gave immature and impulsive adolescents the power of veto over the decisions of adults. His commitment to community involvement ignored the practical impossibility of helping a boy in the same environment that had made him delinquent, and his opposition to "locking up kids" had left his department a paper tiger.

Habitual offenders who refused DYS's help were briefly and reluctantly detained in lockups such as Roslindale, where residence was a source of status. Having no authority to force a kid to accept placement and no means of dealing with him if he didn't, DYS had become, as Fat Jack put it, a "travel agent," trying to sell its clients on the virtues of particular placements. "The way it works," explained our bulbous delinquent one morning at breakfast, "is whenever I get busted, I go down to DYS to look through the brochures. Who knows? They may have somethin' that I like! If the program ain't no good, what the hell? I can always split! . . . You guys is doin' all right," he assured us with an expansive grin. "I'm gonna recommend you to my friends."

As far as Fat Jack and his friends were concerned, Penikese was not an alternative to lockup but an alternative to home.

I had by now experience enough with DYS to know what the system needed to make it work. Accountability was the missing ingredient in Miller's reform. Our job was to prepare kids for a world that would judge them by what they did rather than why they did it. A delinquent's behavior was inevitably impulsive. We had to teach him to think in terms of consequences, and the only way to do this was through a consistently imposed system of rewards and punishments.

Humanely run detention facilities were a necessary part of this effort. I agreed with the reformers that most DYS kids did not belong in lockup, but Fat Jack and many others like him had persuaded me that the threat of confinement was necessary to make them accept less coercive alternatives. I knew a lot of other kids, Mark and Harvey among them, who for their sake as well as society's, needed to be locked up to protect them from their own dangerous impulsiveness. To do anything less was simply to give them the rope to hang themselves, and it made me grind my teeth that in the name of humanitarian reform DYS was doing just that.

What should I do about it? The most direct way to influence DYS policies was obviously political. Miller had accomplished his reforms through political action, and if I believed strongly enough in the need for further change, then wasn't I duty bound to launch my own crusade to make the system work? I suppose I was, but I didn't have it in me to leave a life I enjoyed and go up to Boston to become a political activist. Instead I confined myself to haranguing hapless DYS officials and writing seldom-read prescriptions for improving the department in our annual reports. Like Leavey, I took the easy way out.

13

O N JANUARY 7, 1976, the seven boys who returned from their Christmas holiday to begin the school's first winter term on Penikese found the snowy owl behind the barn and seals in the harbor. Everyone was in high spirits.

Short days and hard weather kept us inside the house a good deal of the time, and Jay Tashiro found it easier to get kids to "do school." He encouraged his scholars to keep journals in which they recorded daily events and whatever else came to mind. Steve, our most conscientious scribe, was a worldly Italian kid who even in the dead of winter affected unbuttoned shirts and a heavy gold chain around his neck. His entry for January 7 rather surprised me. "We came back," he wrote, "to the place which had been my home for three months and would be my home again. It was beginning to feel like I was back where I wanted to be."

Our semiformal educational program added a new dimension to the island. David described an eager but ignorant new boy named Benny who arrived that winter as "an empty bucket just waiting to be filled up." The analogy was an apt one to describe the bright, curious kids who had grown up in a cultural vacuum and who, often for the first time in their lives, voluntarily sat down in front of a book on Penikese. We got our share of Bennys on Penikese, and it was exciting to watch them absorbing new information like sponges.

The absence of television more than anything else helped Jay lure kids into the school house. Even so, our resident pedagogue had to proceed very gingerly not to spook his students. We rarely saw a delinquent who had been successful in school. A record that noted simply that so-and-so had repeated third grade three times did not tell of the horrible moments of embarrassed panic, the countless trips to the principal's office and the constant ridicule from classmates lying behind that statistic. By the time boys who had known nothing but shame and failure got to Penikese, just mentioning the word "school" was often enough to turn them off.

So Jay learned to move slowly. Pushing too hard or too fast inevitably triggered the same defense mechanism a boy had developed in his previous school. Whatever it was—anger, skylarking or simply tuning out—there would be no more teaching possible until Jay had very carefully reeled him back in again.

The secret was not to insist on perfection. Getting a kid to write something—anything—was more important than insisting on the fine points of grammar or spelling. Anyone visiting our rustic school house was likely to find a burly seventeen-year-old with his face screwed up in concentration laboriously shaping the kind of clumsy block letters typical of first-grade posters. Childlike handwriting, however, did not necessarily express childlike sentiments.

Kevin, a boy with a constant scowl, produced a poem he called "Winter Skies":

> Echos of the night
> bodies of the late
> children of yesterday
> days pass like years
> searching for light
>
> Tomorrow might never be
> Moonless modern for a time
> blackness all around in the sky
> nightly senseless, chills
> winds howling uncontrollably
>
> Madness, everywhere, no sanity in sight
>
> No longer anger, just a sound
> from the sky which kills anything
> that is alive.

Tommy, who had a natural talent for the guitar, wrote "I'm Just A Boy," which Yara helped him set to music:

Life seems so long—but yet it's short.
And I'm just a boy in a large world,
Misguided—mistreated. Oh! I don't know
A young boy must hide under his mama's wings,
Until nature tells her to let him go.

Fly away! Fly away to where you're needed.
Take a stand; but be a man,
Because you're free to be
What you want to be.
You're on your own now.
Go and make your home and settle down.

Mama, I'm coming home to stay,
Won't you meet me half way?
Cause there's nothing better I'd like to see
Than mama and me embraced as one
Under the sun.

So won't you fly away
Up high
Under the starry sky
And moonlight glow?

Tommy never got to be the man he sang about. He was killed in a car accident shortly after leaving Penikese.

Roy told of "A Place Where I Was Happy":

I was happy in Unionville. I was happy every day. I knew the paths through the woods and everything. I had a good time every day. We still had some bucks then. My parents got to stay in the house because they took care of the dogs. It was a dog farm—they were collies. They sold puppies for 100 bucks or more. We took care of the dogs every day.

There was a pond there. My mother would put on big boots and clean it out every once in a while. There was a mountain all around the back of the pond. There were squirrels there. Sometimes we'd go up there with our lunches and munch out. There was a store a little way down the road. I remember Unionville. I can see it all.

I know if I got there I'd know everything. That's what I'm gonna do, I'm gonna get a car and go there as soon as I can. Maybe I'll take my brothers and sisters.

There was a house nearby that you could walk to on a path, through the woods, or you could go in a car. We used to go there every day. There was a girl there. We used to go to a place with a big barn full of hay and slide on the hay. The girl found a hole she could slide down and come out a big window on the side of the barn and land on another pile of hay outside. I never could find the hole. The girl had beautiful blond hair. I went there alone once to find the girl's tunnel in the hay barn. I snuck in there and there was no hay. The barn was empty. I couldn't believe it. I felt weird. I went to the house and there were Armenians there! The people who had lived there had moved away. They sold the place to the Armenians. I don't know what happened to the hay. Then my father had his accident. His leg was busted bad. There's a picture of the car wrapped around a tree—all the way around!—Maybe he wasn't drunk. I don't know if he was drunk. He was a carpenter, we had some houses once. Then my brother got sick. They must have had to sell the houses to pay the medical bills.

I didn't even know the word, fuck, when we moved to fuckin' Worcester. My parents got divorced in Worcester. That really sucked!

When I get a car that's what I'm gonna do. I'm gonna go back there. I know I'd know how to go right to my house. I could show you how to get there. I know the paths through the woods and everything. I could build a little house up on that mountain. I'll go see if the Armenians are still there. I'll see if the dog farm is still there. I sure hope that girl is there. She had beautiful blond hair. That's what I'm gonna do. I'm gonna go back there!

When weather permitted working outside, Jack Simonds taught carpentry while building a new chicken house. This turned out to be a controversial project since the location he chose blocked the view from the outhouse. Work stopped while our artistic faction extolled the spiritual value of watching moonrises from the "throne" while the more practically minded among us argued for the convenience of keeping the chickens near the barn. Expediency eventually prevailed over esthetics, and Jack and his crew resumed their labors.

David had the duty on February 2. "This was the wildest Ground-hog Day I can remember," he wrote in his daily log. "Jack and I were awakened by the sound of the howling wind at 5:45, just in time to see the cistern roof come sailing down the hill and land in the garden. The house itself was shaking from the force of the gale. Buzzards Bay's entrance tower was reporting a steady 70 mile an hour wind, gusting to 92 miles per hour. All three skiffs, high on what is normally the beach, were awash in the surf. We managed to haul the two small skiffs out, but lost the large one. It was brutally cold — about 10 degrees, and God knows what the chill factor was. Back at the house we nailed the front door shut, and rebraced the north wall. The tide was over the dock, and large waves on the lee side of the Island were breaking over into the pond and eroding the high beach road. Over on the windward side it was impossible to stand on the edge of the cliff. The sun came out briefly, illuminating a wonderfully wild sea, and then the blizzard returned to reduce the visibility to about 100 feet. Sixteen hours later the wind continued unabated."

March brought with it the first glimmers of spring. The gulls returned to Penikese in such numbers that from daybreak until dark the island rang with the sounds of their incessant crying and squabbling. Canada geese built their nests, and our two impertinent young sows began making indecent advances on their keepers.

My advertisement in the local paper for a boar was answered by a pig farmer on Martha's Vineyard, so on my way back from Penikese one afternoon I stopped off at Menemsha to meet our prospective bridegroom. "He's still awful small," I told the seller. "We're hoping to breed this spring".

"Not to worry," he assured me. "Love will find a way."

I took his word for it and returned to Penikese with a very sea-sick little black pig whom the kids promptly named Arnold, why I don't know. Arnold proved to be brilliant at getting out of his pen, but he showed no apparent interest in the ladies, so we reconciled ourselves sadly to having no piglets that summer.

As the days grew longer, outside projects again began to occupy most of our time. We built a new roof for the cistern, enlarged the pigpen, spread compost on the garden and launched our first island-built boat. I had prefabricated the parts for this little lapstrake skiff in my shop at home, and the kids assembled them on the island. They were proud of the boat, and so was I.

David, meanwhile, was beginning work on our garden. In April the kids planted peas and began our annual war against the rabbits. The four hundred strawberry plants we put in later that month did well until Paul, the very disturbed son of a psychiatrist, was assigned to weed the strawberry patch. He pulled up all the strawberries along with the weeds.

On August 10, three months, three weeks and three days following our little boar's arrival on Penikese, our doubts about Arnold were dispelled when both sows farrowed and our pig population jumped to twenty-three. Love *had* found a way!

Jack Simonds, Jay Tashiro, Dickey Edwards and Caroline "Crow" Smith all left us within a few months of each other that fall. None of them had joined the staff intending to stay as long as they had, but Penikese had worked its magic on them as well. They were all in their early twenties and had other careers to go on to. The two years they had given us (three for Jack) were nearly unprecedented at a time when the staff at other DYS programs seldom lasted more than six months before burning out. I hated to see them go.

Herman Bosch's departure at the end of the year to go back to sea left me with another big hole to fill. Following our fiasco on Cuttyhunk he had gradually removed himself from involvement with the kids and taken on more of the job of administering the school. Technically he and I shared the job of maintaining student records, handling payroll, filing reports and keeping our creditors at bay, but in fact Herman did most of this work. After he left I found myself so swamped with paperwork during my time off the island that I had even less time than before to spend with my own family.

The new staff members who joined the school in 1976 were all older than the people they replaced. Sue Heywood, who took Crow's place, was a blond, no-nonsense woman who soon had all the kids eating out of her hand. On her time off she sang at local night spots, and on the island she used her powerful voice to good effect. One day while I was standing outside the house I heard a mighty roar from within and looked up to see kids exploding out every open door and window. Seconds later Sue burst out the porch door, pursuing some laggard with a broom. I never found out what the kids did to upset her, but I'll bet it was a long time before any of them ever tried to do it again.

Jay's replacement, Phil Westra, had the misfortune to look so much like me that we were often mistaken for brothers. Before coming to Penikese, Phil had set up a remedial-education program at DYS's secure facility in Roslindale, a job he quit in disgust. "Kids can't learn in a place like that" he told me. "They're too busy just trying to survive." What he liked best about the island was the absence of fear. "At Roslindale the meanest psychopath is the king shit," said Phil. "I knew things were different on Penikese when one of my stars at arithmetic evidently felt threatened by a new kid who said he could do algebra."

John McRoberts and Otto Reber were both part of a migration of talented Lycoming College graduates who for one reason or another had fetched up in Falmouth. The two of them had experimented with various careers before ending up as first-rate carpenters. John could have been a movie star and was a great hand with the ladies, while Otto looked like the wrestler he had been in college. They were instinctive teachers and unflappable in emergencies, which was and is a valuable asset for anyone who works at Penikese.

With this much new talent, I was no longer needed as a shift leader. So late in 1976 I took myself off the watch schedule to devote full time to running the office and the boat. This arrangement gave me more nights at home and about the same number of days on the island, since the two or three trips down I made every week worked out to nearly the same amount of time I had spent there when working alternate full-week shifts.

With Herman gone, I was forced to pay more attention to the business end of our operation and, whenever I studied our books, I was confronted with irrefutable evidence that the Penikese Island School needed to get bigger. Six to eight students, which after three years of experimenting appeared to be our optimum enrollment from an operational standpoint, was too small a number to ensure any kind of financial stability. Whenever we lost a boy unexpectedly (which was usually how we lost him), a big chunk of our operating income went with him until DYS sent us a replacement.

Because of the frantic way most regional DYS offices operated, we were never able to keep a waiting list of applicants. If we could not take a boy within a few days of receiving his application, he went somewhere else. Further delays in filling vacancies were cranked in by the logistic problems involved in getting to the island and the need for caution in screening applicants for what was unquestionably the most accident-prone environment to which DYS kids were then being sent.

Raising our enrollment to twenty or so boys would provide sufficient critical mass to cushion the effects of these various constraints. My financial projections told me that even if we increased staff by the same proportion as students we would still come out ahead. Since overhead remained more-or-less constant, even eight staff with ten students looked better on the books than six staff and eight students.

I decided to talk this idea over with David, who as the last of the old guard still with Penikese, had become pretty much my partner in running the school. So on a day when neither one of us was on the island I stopped by his house, filled with excitement about grandiose schemes for expansion.

"Be right up," David hollered from his garden as I waded through the sea of cats he for some contradictory reason kept around despite his love for birds. A one-eared tomcat arched his back and hissed.

"Watch that one," warned David. "He'll rub up against your leg one minute and scratch the shit out of you the next."

"Just like Peter's father," I replied, thinking of one of our more troubled students. "Poor kid never knows if his dad's going to whip him or take him to the ballgame."

"Yeah," said David. "That's the one common denominator to all Penikese kids. They never know what the hell to expect."

He was right. I thought of Duane the night I found him at his house with his mercurial mother, of Peter whose caseworker had sent him to us for "excessive car stealing" and of Robert whose dad boasted that "even the gym teacher's afraid of my kid" and then demanded the state's help with his belligerent son. Those three kids really did live in a nightmare world of conflicting signals. Whether they were praised, punished or ignored depended more on the erratic mood of unstable adults or on the equally erratic intervention of officialdom than on anything they did themselves.

I had heard a former POW who lectured us at Quantico describe an experience that seemed startlingly similar to the ones delinquents confronted every day, and I found myself telling David how the Chinese in Korea had brainwashed American prisoners. I told him how men had lived in cells without windows where the lights had come on and off at random intervals, how four meals in four hours would be followed by none for a week, how right answers at one interrogation had been wrong answers at the next, and how even strong men had come unglued in this completely random environment.

"Our gang has it worse," said David. "If it's bad to be randomly praised or beaten by someone you know is your enemy, it's got to be worse when the person doing it is your father or mother. No wonder Penikese kids are such fatalists. If everything they do leads to unforeseeable consequences, I guess they figure they might as well do anything they damn well feel like—or else nothing at all. Remember, back when we started, how Nick used to say he knew he was going to jail, and we all tried to convince him that he could stay straight if he wanted to? No wonder he didn't believe us."

"Maybe that's why that kid went after the chickens," I speculated. "If you feel completely out of control, you're going to resent it, and resentment leads to the kind of anger you can't even focus on anything specific so you just lash out at whatever happens to be around you. I guess those chickens were just in the wrong place at the wrong time."

"Makes sense, I guess," David said. "But I think it takes more than just a confusing environment to create a real psychopath, and that kid was one. My guess is that it was Scott."

"Scott? Maybe so. He certainly looked the part. At any event, we better not get back on that one or we'll never get to the subject at hand."

"Oh? And what is the subject at hand?"

"Expansion. We've got to get bigger. A lot bigger."

"Great! First we decide we've got to concentrate on showing our kids that what they do has some influence on what happens to them, and now you propose to turn the island into a huge zoo where all our students get lost in the shuffle. Way it is now, a kid can see when he doesn't cut enough wood that the house is cold. It's lessons like that that may begin to show him that he can control his future. You get much bigger, and those kind of simple things become much less obvious."

"What I propose is to generate enough income to keep the damn place going."

"You'll have to find some other way. Getting bigger won't work. We've built sort of a family down there, and we can't lose that. For most of our kids their time with us is going to be as close to a decent family life as they ever get. You and I are fathers, John, Otto and Phil are older brothers, Molly's an older sister and Sue? I guess Sue is a mother and a sister. She covers all the bases."

David was right. The boot-camp model I had started out with seemed less and less relevant. We had to teach self-confidence — I was right about that — but the kind of confidence our kids needed had nothing to do with mastering physical challenges. They were already better than most in that department. They needed to learn the kind of confidence David had been talking about: the confidence that came from knowing they could run their own show. If we could teach them that, we'd have done our job, but to do it we would have to stay small enough for every kid on Penikese to be a very visible member of the group.

14

AFTER GOING OFF the watch schedule I still tried to spend a few nights each month on Penikese, but since I usually had people to bring in whenever I took anyone out, this did not always work as planned. Consequently I saw the staff and kids most frequently during my three or so trips each week to the island.

Most of the kids liked to "drive" the boat, and I discovered there was a pretty good correlation between how readily a new boy mastered steering by compass and how well he was likely to do on Penikese. Some took to it immediately. Others could not concentrate long enough to stay on course, and still others (usually those with reading problems) just could not get the idea that the lubber line moved relative to the numbers instead of vice versa.

After unsuccessfully trying various ways to explain this principle, I hit pay dirt by describing the compass as a video game. I had the kids visualize an imaginary road running through the number indicating the course. The lubber line was their racing car, and the driver's job was to keep his car on the road. To add excitement to this game another boy armed with a length of broom handle was stationed behind the driver. Any time the racing car strayed more than five degrees "into the ditch" on either side of the assigned course, the driver got poked in the ass. In order to keep things from getting out of hand, driver and poker then rotated jobs.

Occasionally a boy got seriously interested in piloting. His curiosity was generally infectious enough to get others involved, so then I would assign masters and mates. First the master drove while the mate navigated, and then they would switch. Interest increased over the years as we added radar and then loran. Charts, dividers, and parallel rules, the traditional tools of the pilot, were too much like school, but TV-like screens and flashing numbers never failed to generate interest.

Winter trips were sometimes nightmares. Even Eisenhower before D-Day could not have agonized more than I did over the decision to go or not go in marginal conditions. Emergencies were easier to handle because then I had no choice. Routine shift changes or trips to bring kids in for their weekends were another story. Waiting meant leaving three tired staff and a lot of unhappy kids on the island. Going could lead to smashing up the boat, getting somebody's leg caught between the rail and the pier, or worse. Prudence dictated waiting. Knowing what the kids' reaction to a postponed weekend would be was a powerful incentive to go. I usually went and then wished I hadn't.

When gale warnings were up, what I dreaded most was a late-night call from the Marine Operator. That usually meant a boat ride. So when the phone rang one Saturday evening just as my family and I were leaving for the movies, I suspected the worst. Sure enough Otto Reber was on the line, radioing in via the New Bedford Marine Operator to report that Pedro was complaining of stomach pains and should come in. I could hear the other kids laughing in the background while he was talking, so I doubted if Otto was at liberty to give me the full details of this latest development in a week during which Pedro had been an unremitting pain in the ass. On the other hand, if Pedro hadn't been a pain in the ass he probably wouldn't be on Penikese in the first place.

We have an unwritten understanding that we will take a kid off the island any time the staff on duty requests it, and Otto was not one to take advantage of this policy, particularly on a night like that one. I expected Pedro was coming in for reasons other than his health, and I would be very surprised if he didn't run as soon as I got him back to Woods Hole.

There were lamentations from my own two boys when they learned that they would not be going to the movies after all. I told them that we would go next Saturday, but I could see from their faces that they didn't believe me. I had let them down too often.

Yara would normally have taken them without me, but that night she had lost her glasses and couldn't drive, which was probably just as well, since the Weather Service had posted travelers' advisories as well as gale warnings. It was still wet, foggy and unusually warm for late November, but later that evening a front was scheduled to come through, bringing with it such cold air that the roads were expected to be icy by midnight. It looked like I would have fog on the way out and wind on the way back.

I grabbed my bag of foul-weather gear, created a bad-tempered crisis by losing my hat, and departed for the Oceanographic pier where we kept our boat. The night watchman there was an old friend.

"You going down *tonight?*" he asked.

I feigned nonchalance. "Shouldn't be too bad. I've got the radar."

Actually, I might not have the radar. On my last trip the picture had kept fading, and once, while fiddling with the gain, I had lost it altogether. I hoped this wouldn't happen again.

The boat's big diesel lit off with a satisfying roar. I switched on the radar and, while waiting for the engine to warm up, walked out to the end of the pier to see if I could make out the Grassy Island Light.

The fog was so thick I couldn't see it, even though it was only five hundred yards away. What wind there was was southeast. The current was flooding, which meant I would make better time going down Buzzards Bay than I would in Vineyard Sound where the easterly flood would be running hard against me. I also knew the bay better if the radar crapped out.

The slip we rented from the Oceanographic opened onto the narrow Eel Pond Channel at an angle that made leaving it awkward, particularly if the wind was blowing with any strength from the south. After a long period of timid backing and filling every time we left the dock, I finally figured out that by putting the wheel hard right and gunning the engine at the right moment, I could get around the corner in one shot without smashing into the stone wall on the far side of the channel. To the uninitiated this maneuver was a startling one, and I must admit that I sometimes enjoyed terrifying the various state functionaries who invited themselves on summertime junkets to Penikese by roaring out of the slip, apparently headed for certain doom. That night there was no one to terrify except myself, so I made a more leisurely departure.

Evidently one of the Steamship Authority ferries docked nearby had its radar running, because mine was picking up too much interference to be much use. I hugged the east side of the Oceanographic pier, instinctively reluctant to leave the security of knowing where I was, and then came to the course which should have brought me in sight of the still invisible Grassy Island Light. Almost instantly the boat was engulfed by the fog. It's not often that from anywhere within the small triangle of water formed by the Oceanographic, the Steamship Authority pier and Grassy Island you can't make out the lights of at least one of them, but that night I could see only the reflection of my own running lights.

I crept along, dead slow. Where the hell was Grassy Island? I was about to backtrack to the Oceanograhic and start out all over again when I felt the boat jerk around in the flood-tide eddy I knew was just east of the island, and I looked up to see the light blinking faintly ahead. Now I would have to be careful not to run down the nun buoy that is just south of it. There it was, its white Number 2, glistening wetly with the reflection of the light. My course from there was due west to the spindle where the channel divided.

There was a moon tide that night, and the current was running very hard through the Hole. I passed buoy Number 4 close enough to see a wake of white water pouring past it. The boat yawed about in the grip of racing eddies, and for a couple of minutes I had my hands full trying to hold the course on the compass while at the same time keeping an eye out for the light on the spindle.

By the time I spotted it, the radar had come back into focus and was painting a fairly good picture of the line of three nuns that led out of the channel. I passed each one close aboard and then came right to 335 degrees, heading for the flashing green light on can Number 13. To get there I would have to pass Number 11, which was not lit and was not painting on the radar. I had visions of running into the damn thing but evidently passed it sight unseen because there was Number 13, its light making a pretty green halo in the fog.

From Number 13 I had a straight shot down the bay with only the little Weepecket islands to avoid for the next ten miles. I came left again to 154 and set off at seven knots.

Before we got the radar, I had carefully plotted and timed every leg of the journey to Penikese, so I always knew with reasonable accuracy where I was. Despite good intentions to continue this practice, the radar had made me sloppy, and I now relied almost entirely on its picture to navigate with. That night I resolved to be more careful and so ducked down below to get the alarm clock I used as a timer. It was not on its shelf, and a frantic search failed to turn it up anywhere else. Swearing, I ran back up to the wheel before we drifted too far off course. The cursor was still revolving methodically around the radar screen, and the radius rings glowed brightly, but there was no picture.

I backed off on the Sea Return button and nudged up the Gain but got nothing. Maybe if I let it cool off the picture would come back. I switched it off and watched the light on the screen shrink into a tiny point in the center and then disappear. With no clock and no radar, I debated whether to turn around and try to feel my way back into Woods Hole but decided to go on. The fog would lift when the front came through, so if I got too badly screwed up I could always anchor and wait for it to clear. A knot begain to tie itself in my stomach.

We were getting pretty close to the Weepeckets. The fathometer indicated shoaling water, and I came left a bit to follow the twenty-foot curve around the southern tip of the island. When the depth began to drop off again I came back to 260 which with luck would in another forty minutes or so put me in sight of the flashing green light on the Lone Rock Buoy off of Quick's Hole. There was nothing much to do until then but "go for it" as the kids say. I wondered if one of those maggots stole my clock. I bet one had.

The book says the right speed in reduced visibility is whatever is "reasonable and proper" for the prevailing conditions. With zero visibility and no radar, it was debatable if any speed was "reasonable and proper," but nonetheless I found myself inching forward on the throttle in my anxiety to find Lone Rock. It was not likely that there were any other boats out that night in the upper bay, but

I had to be careful approaching the Quick's Hole channel, as I imagined some of the New Bedford fishing fleet would be hightailing it in ahead of the blow that was coming.

I tried the radar once again and got a fleeting picture of Crescent Beach at the west end of Naushon before the image faded again. That was reassuring. I was more or less where I figured I ought to be, and if I could count on the damn radar for an occasional picture, I wouldn't have too much trouble finding my way in to Penikese.

Was that a green flash? I slowed down and I stared intently into the darkness but didn't see it again. Not to worry. Green lights have . a habit of appearing and disappearing when seen from a distance. I would go on for another ten minutes, and if I still didn't spot it, then I'd start worrying. Visibility would be better if it weren't for the reflected glare of my own forward range light on the wheelhouse roof. I slowed down again and climbed forward to cover it with my hat. Evidently I had put in too big a bulb when I last replaced it.

While I was up on the foredeck, the boat swung broadside to the seas and rolled heavily. Here in the lower bay the east wind had kicked up quite a swell which I knew would make it hard to get in to our pier at Penikese. The wind itself had dropped off to just about nothing, so that front wasn't too far away.

I cranked up again and soon had the Lone Rock Light in sight. The fog seemed to be thinning a bit as it often did around Quick's. I saw no fishing boats so steamed right up to the light, from where I took my course to the next lighted marker, halfway down Nashawena Island.

Fifteen minutes went by, and I still didn't see the Nashawena Light. I tried the radar but got no picture. Damn! I must be right on top of the thing. I knew the Coast Guard hauled up this marker before ice season, but I couldn't believe they would have hauled it this early. It seemed to me it had been there the day before, but Friday had been a bright, clear day, and I hadn't been paying much attention.

I was milling around trying to figure out what to do next when I spotted a very dim light off to port. It faded away as I looked at it and then reappeared briefly through a fleeting rift in the fog. That had to be the Nashawena farmhouse. Thank God Ann and Alan Wilder, who live there, were up late. The Gull Island Shoal had to be right ahead, so I decided to poke in towards the Nashawena shore and then work my way around Knox Point on the fathometer. When I spotted the lighted entrance bell to Cuttyhunk Harbor I would head from there more or less due north to Penikese.

I proceeded with this plan. Eventually a dull yellow halo in the fog told me that Cuttyhunk was ahead. While looking for the bell I nearly ran over it. It was only a mile from here to Penikese. I headed a little to the right of north to compensate for the current, which was now running to the west.

There was only a relatively narrow stretch of good water leading into our harbor. I had made this trip so often that I thought I could hit the entrance easily enough unless I badly misjudged the current. I wasn't so sure I could get into the pier without blundering onto one of the rocks that lie around it. I wished I had thought to ask Otto to hang a lantern from a piling.

I ran along at seven knots for what I estimated to be five minutes and then throttled back to dead slow while setting up a huge racket on the horn in hopes of bringing someone down to the beach. Two more minutes went by. I played another concert on the horn, and then I was nearly blinded by a powerful flashlight shining in the cabin window. Good old Otto!

As always with an east wind, there was a heavy surge slopping up against the stone jetty that served as our pier. I nosed in and Otto jumped aboard. Behind him on the rocks I could make out the silhouettes of our newest staff member, Paul Dixon, and the infamous Pedro, their faces grotesque in the flickering shadows from a kerosene lantern. Otto wanted to talk. We backed off again rather than risk lying against the stone jetty.

"Hi, Otto."

"Hi, George," said Otto, a solid presence in the dark.

"Rough trip?"

"Sort of. Radar crapped out. Fog's some thick."

"Yeah, I guess. Jeez, I'm sorry to bring you down in this stuff, but we really got to get this guy off before someone gets hurt. Friday he winged a hammer at Mark, and yesterday he would have gone after Sue with a knife if Paul hadn't grabbed him."

"Is he really sick?"

"Sick? I dunno. I think he knew we were going to have to can him. Maybe he's just trying to save face with the rest of the gang by going off sick, but, if so, it's a pretty good act. He hasn't eaten all day which isn't like him. . . . You know how he eats. He won't let me take his temperature. . . . I dunno. We were going to let things slide until you got down on Monday, but then I heard the weather and he started moaning about appendicitis, so I figured we'd better get him off while we still could. . . . I was planning to radio in anyway tonight to see if you could set it up to have DYS pick him up Monday."

"I think you made the right call. Gale warnings are already up, and it's supposed to blow like hell for the next couple of days, so I won't be able to get down Monday if that forecast is even close to right. . . . Don't know what I'm going to do with Pedro until I can get hold of DYS. . . . No way they'll pick him up on Sunday."

"Maybe he really does have appendicitis," Otto said hopefully.

"More likely he'll run. Well, I better get going. It'll be a slow trip back. Can I borrow your watch? Somebody's stole my clock."

"Sure. Paul's got you a cup of coffee. Probably cold by now. We were waiting quite a while. I'll get it."

"Thanks. Pedro got all his stuff?"

"Yeah. He knows he's not coming back. I had a talk with him. I feel kinda sorry for the poor guy. In his own way he tried, but Jesus Christ, the kid's an animal. He was ruining it here for all the others."

Otto went forward to help Pedro with his duffle bag. As I nosed back into the pier I saw Paul and Pedro shake hands. Then Pedro jumped aboard, and he and Otto came running aft as I jockeyed to hold the boat away from the rocks.

Otto handed me the coffee, slapped Pedro on the shoulder and jumped to the pier as I backed off.

"Hi, Pedro. How you feeling?"

"Feel like shit, man. My gut's all screwed up."

"Otto tell you why you're coming off?"

"Yeah. 'Cause I called Sue a bitch."

"That all?"

"Naw, I done some other stuff too."

I was too busy trying to keep track of where we were to continue this conversation. Pedro knelt beside me on the engine box. We ran due south for six minutes and then came left to 080. Sure nice to have a watch. Pedro said something that I didn't hear over the engine.

"What?"

"Gonna miss Otto and Paul. They're alright." He grinned. "Gonna miss Sue too, even if she is a bitch."

He slumped back on the engine box. A couple of minutes later he was up again looking around.

"How do you know where you are?" he asked.

"I don't. Thought you did."

"Man, I couldn't find my own asshole out here."

Halfway along Nashawena we ran into a furious squall which Pedro slept right through. The wind slammed around to the north, shredding the fog before it, and the bay and islands stood revealed in the dazzling light of the cold, full moon.

"Hey, Pedro. Look at this."

He looked around, sleepy eyed and unimpressed, then went back to sleep. Clouds raced across the sky. Whitecaps flashed above the wind-whipped water. Pedro's nonchalance in the face of all this majesty reminded me of the fall night years ago when I was plugging down the bay in our old *Nereis* with all the kids asleep below. A giant orange harvest moon had risen from behind Naushon, and I woke them up to see it. Everyone had been profanely annoyed at being disturbed "just to see the fuckin' moon" except for little Keith, who had stood transfixed at the spectacle. Two years later, Keith had wandered back to Woods Hole, his mind almost entirely destroyed by drugs, but still able to remember that moon.

It was really piping up. I decided I'd better duck through Quick's and look for a lee on the other side of the islands. We turned downwind with a big following sea making up behind us and scooted through the hole into the comparative calm of Vineyard Sound.

The rest of the trip was uneventful. Passing Robinson's Hole, I noticed that Freddy Gaskell's lights were still on. Seemed that all of the islanders were up late that night. Freddy was the only resident on Pasque Island. He was dying of emphysema but refused to be taken off, preferring to end his days alone. Some night, perhaps on a night like this one, I expected he would just nod off by his kerosene lantern and never wake again.

Pedro was stirring.

"Hey, Pedro, you know what happened to my clock?"

"Yeah. Reggie copped it the day he graduated. Took a flare, too."

In the peculiar ethical system of the kids, Pedro would never fink on Reggie as long as the two of them were still together on the island. But now that Reggie had left, his former friend had no compunctions about informing on him. I wondered if for our kids anything really existed except the immediate present. For Pedro I expect the memory of Reggie had become just another among the random mental images that whirled incoherently about in his head.

I had been at this business long enough that I should not have been disappointed at learning that Reggie had stolen my clock. He was one of our star students, the kind of kid we liked to think about when attempting to reassure ourselves that our work here was accomplishing something. On the day he left, Sue baked him a huge cake, and the staff all chipped in to buy him a graduation present. Then he jumped onto the boat and stole the clock.

There was a solitary sailboat anchored in Tarpaulin Cove, where, if the skipper was smart, he would ride out the next couple of days. I guessed he had made a late start heading south, and I imagined he was going to get at least one good dusting before he reached warm weather.

Rounding the east end of Naushon into Woods Hole, we were hit by the full force of the north wind. Salt spray on the windscreen began to freeze. The temperature must have dropped forty degrees in the last hour. "Jesus fuckin' freezin'!" announced Pedro poetically.

We backed into the slip and tied up with numb hands. I asked Pedro if he was going to run, but he only grinned, so we made a slippery trip to the hospital where he was diagnosed as having intestinal flu. He spent Sunday recuperating at my house, and on Monday I drove him up to the DYS lockup in Taunton. When I left him there he was crying.

15

A MONG THE FIRST GROUP to winter over was Randy, who came to Penikese after bombing out of twelve previous DYS placements. Randy's father had abandoned him. His older brother had killed himself, a loss his mother never recovered from. This succession of tragedies left Randy withdrawn and, in the opinion of the court psychologist, incapable of feelings or visible emotion.

Initially it seemed that way to us also. Randy kept to himself and woodenly went about doing exactly what he was asked, no more and no less. His immense strength commanded enough respect that the other kids did not venture to intrude on his privacy. Gradually he began to come out of his shell. Rather than retreat immediately to bed after dinner he set up the chess set and waited quietly for someone to play him. He usually won.

One blustery January day Yara came down with her accordion and our two boys for an overnight visit and ended up spending a week during which the wind never let up enough to run a boat. Not even the most bashful vocalist can long resist Yara's accordion, and she soon had the gang making the rafters ring with discordant renditions of old Beatles songs. Loudest of all was Randy's booming baritone. He was almost beside himself with delight, capering about between songs and shouting for more until Yara finally collapsed under the weight of her ponderous instrument, and the crew went off hoarse and happy to bed. So much, I thought, for that boy's incapacity for emotion.

Randy was built like a fireplug and with his great moon of a face reminded me of Pavarotti, whose voice he could match at least in volume. I recall walking up from the pier early in the spring to find him on the tractor harrowing the garden. As I heard him bellowing "Yellow Submarine" above the sound of the engine and saw him cutting great arcs through the newly turned soil, it occurred to me I was watching a completely happy person.

Our new extrovert was capable of enormous enthusiasms and equally great disappointments. He would set difficult goals for himself and then be filled with despair when he fell short of the mark. His ambition was to join the Marine Corps. As his four-month stay on Penikese neared its end, we crammed him furiously for the Armed Forces Aptitude Test and exercised him equally furiously to shed his formidable paunch. With constant encouragement he could keep his nose to the wheel. Left to his own devices he became discouraged and quit. We gave him constant encouragement. When he was not huffing laboriously around our running track we made sure he was hard at work on the books.

On the appointed day we presented our slimmed-down, fact-filled candidate to the recruiter. Randy knew that only a good score on the aptitude test would lead the Marines to overlook his juvenile record. He locked up under the pressure. Nothing went right. He was tongue-tied during his interview and missed questions on the test that were identical to ones he had studied. Watching the poor kid flounder, I realized we had tried to push him too far too fast, and I hoped this disappointment would not drive him back into his shell.

It didn't. Once Randy was back on the island his funk gave way to a new enthusiasm. This time he wanted to be a long-distance truck driver. Out came the road atlas. We were regaled with lyric accounts of the open road. The names of far-away places rolled off his tongue. "Hey, get this one! Blue Balls, Pennsylvania. I'm gonna drive my rig to Blue Balls, you wait and see!"

Driving to Blue Balls seemed like an achievable goal. Leo Cohen had a friend in the moving business who agreed to talk to Randy. I drove him up to Quincy, outside Boston, where under a sign that said Avoid Spring Cleaning. Move Out! we found the office of Carroll the Mover.

After our interview with Dick Carroll, I was every bit as enthusiastic as Randy. Moving, it seemed, was one field where ex-cons and school dropouts stood a chance. Many of Dick's crew had records. The teenage helpers he hired each year who worked out could expect to be earning $20,000 a year and driving their own trucks by age twenty-one. Education wasn't important, "busting ass" was. So was initiative. Dick showed Randy one of his Helper Evaluation Reports. Two questions were underlined.

Does he have to be told to do everything?   Yes_____ No_____
Does he dodge the heavy pieces?   Yes_____ No_____

"Get a 'no' for both of those," said Dick, "and you're on your way in the moving business."

I looked at Randy and decided that the Good Lord had intended him to move furniture. His sturdy frame might not have been built for forced marches at Parris Island, but he sure as hell could lift the heavy pieces.

We found Randy a room at the YMCA, and he went off euphorically to start a new life. Two weeks later I got a letter from Dick:

Dear George:

I have attached one of Randy's Helper Evaluation Reports. As you can see he is having a tough time in some of his dutys. However I am confident we can turn him around. The things that will tell the story are the two I put in the black marks behind; he has to be told to do everything and he dodges the heavy pieces.

The drivers tell me all he talks about is getting a raise in July. Well, I had a talk with him and explained the facts of life to him. The drivers pay him and if I gave him a raise they would raise my scalp. The drivers will be filling these report out again for July and he has a chance to earn a raise.

I also pointed out to Randy that we put on 6 kids all 17. One got a 50 cent per hour raise because the drivers felt that he deserved it. We find out who is hustling and who is not by the drivers' requests for helpers. If a kid is good they all want him, if a kid is slacking off no one wants him. I told Randy to watch the kid that got the raise. They are the same age. The other kid is smaller. How come?

I think reality has hit him kind of hard but he went home for the weekend and he was back Tuesday so we still have a ballgame. If

I can just motivate him out of the mopy feeling sorry for myself attitude he has now, we got him. Excuse this sloppy letter.

Dick Carroll

I then did a stupid thing. We had a lot riding on Randy's success. Jobs for our graduates were hard to find. If Randy did well, Dick had offered to take on other Penikese kids and to recommend us to his friends in the trucking business. So I went up to Quincy and reamed Randy out for laziness. I was so angry I didn't even notice the change two weeks had made in him. His tan was gone, and his face was pinched. He was plainly miserable, but I knew his capacity for self-pity, and this made me madder yet. "Goddamnit!" I yelled. "Why don't you get off your dead ass? You're ruining something good for you and for us both!"

That said, I stomped indignantly off, leaving Randy with the additional responsibility not "to screw things up for other Penikese kids who may have balls enough to 'lift the heavy pieces.'" To his credit he hung on for two more weeks before he quit.

Randy's collapse made me wonder about the then-popular thesis that the best way to get dropout kids off the street was to put them in interesting jobs which offered them a future. The pendulum was already beginning to swing slowly away from the "touchy-feely" approach to rehabilitation toward a more practical commitment to job training. Word was out that the Law Enforcement Assistance Agency (LEAA) was about to pump millions of dollars into Massachusetts, and DYS's new commissioner, John Calhoun, was already lobbying to see that some of this money went towards programs offering vocational training and job placement for delinquents. What Calhoun was looking for was exactly what we had given Randy. We had come up with what seemed to be an ideal match between boy and job. Why hadn't it worked?

From what I was later able to piece together from Dick Carroll, the people at the Y and Randy himself, it seemed Randy's new life rapidly degenerated into a nightmare. Living entirely alone for the first time in his seventeen years, he slept through breakfast and arrived for work on an empty stomach. He ate junk for lunch and often got back to his lonely room too tired to bother about dinner.

In only a few days he had starved himself to the point where he was no longer hungry. From then on he slept more and ate less until before long he found himself literally unable to lift the heavy pieces.

Other than at work, he spoke to no one for days at a time. His only recreation was swimming in the YMCA pool, but that ended when a girl laughed at the obscene tatoos he had inflicted on himself during one of his long stretches in detention. His personal hygiene, never his strong suit, went so completely to hell that his lethargy was not the only reason his coworkers had begun to avoid him. No wonder the poor kid quit.

Penikese was not producing employable graduates. Randy showed me that. Although our teachers Jay Tashiro and Phil Westra had worked some miracles with our remedial-education program, not many of our kids were ever going to go back to school. For most of them Penikese would be their last chance at an education, either academic or vocational, before they were thrown back on their own resources to compete in an adult world. We had been naive to expect that by itself our island program could adequately prepare them for a new future. It was too much to expect of even the most motivated seventeen-year-old to move directly from a place where somebody got him up in the morning, made sure he ate properly, and kept his nose to the grindstone, into an environment where he had to do everything on his own. We needed some way to help our graduates make the transition from the island to living on their own and working full time.

Conventional wisdom in the midseventies blamed high unemployment among young people on a lack of job opportunities, and the federal government was responding to this perception of the problem by launching the Comprehensive Employment and Training Act (CETA), which turned capitalism upside down by subsidizing jobs that the marketplace would not otherwise create. DYS kids were being given CETA jobs in droves, and the results were not impressive. Although I suppose CETA accomplished some good, most of the jobs created involved either make-work or no work, and the kids that held them came away with the impression that a job was simply another form of handout.

Lack of jobs was not the problem. There were plenty of people like Dick Carroll who were willing to give teenagers a chance. Dropout kids were unemployed because they were unemployable. They lacked the self-discipline to stick to a schedule or keep working when tired. Their sensitivity to being "hassled" made it hard for them to take orders. At best they would do the minimum necessary to get by. At worst they would be an outright liability to an employer. Before they could be given jobs or could learn specific trades, they first had to be taught how to work.

We could make a start at this on the island. Roy's "moles" learned that hard work could be fun, and even Fat Jack performed prodigious labors on occasion. We were not going to turn out master carpenters, chefs, farmers or boat handlers, but we were able to encourage pride in workmanship, initiative, and perseverance. We might even be able to convince our graduates that to succeed they would have to be willing to work harder than job competitors who were older, better educated and better trained.

But we needed something else—a follow-on program on the mainland where island graduates could live under our supervision as they began their working careers and learned how to take care of themselves. This new program could introduce its students to the mysteries of food shopping, personal finances, organizing the day, grooming, washing clothes, eating regular meals, living as nonabrasive members of a community, paying taxes, driving cars (legally), getting enough exercise, using leisure time productively, and all the other requirements of civilized living.

I realized all too well that an operation of this kind was not without risk. Very few community-based DYS contractors were on good terms with their neighbors, and I knew our remote location was one reason we enjoyed so much support in Woods Hole and Falmouth. Moving ashore might change all that. There could be no guarantee that our kids wouldn't run amok when confronted with the temptations of civilization, but at least we would have the advantage of being able to screen candidates for the mainland during the four months they spent on the island.

Jobs were another problem. Falmouth was not big enough to absorb many entrants to the job market and, even if it were, I did not relish the prospect of growing numbers of our graduates taking up permanent residence on the Cape. We would have to find local employers willing to provide what amounted to short-term apprenticeships, at the end of which our students would go on to jobs somewhere else. This raised yet another obstacle. It was hardly fair to ask an employer to put on his payroll a trainee he knew would leave as soon as he became productive. The solution might be for us to provide our students with a stipend while they traded their labor for what their employer could teach them. It seemed to me this version of the old-fashioned apprenticeship had a number of other advantages. Students would remain covered by Penikese's liability insurance, and employers would be spared the additional bookkeeping involved in payroll and withholding. We would also be able to circumvent the Occupational Safety and Health Act, which forbade employees under eighteen from working around machinery but had no such restrictions for unpaid apprentices.

Getting the right kid into the right apprenticeship would be a big part of the job. Our students usually had little conception of their actual aptitudes, and, thanks to CETA, they were wildly unrealistic about their value on the job market. Their job preferences were dictated by glamour, "macho" job stereotypes, and inflated assessments of their own abilities. The sad part was that a boy's perception of what he wanted to do, no matter how unrealistic, was a big part of the fragile fabric of dreams he clung to. A kid who fantasized about racing stock cars would not easily give up his goal of becoming a mechanic even if he had no such aptitude. Ideally our training program would have to have access to a sufficient variety of apprenticeships to allow us to balance desires and abilities well enough to make a good fit. Our incompetent mechanic might find happiness, for example, yanking parts in an auto-salvage yard.

I wasn't sure exactly how we would find our mainland students permanent jobs, but I knew that we should try to avoid CETA and the other avenues normally followed in finding work for DYS kids. If at all possible I wanted our graduates to make a clean start in a work environment far removed from what prevailed in subsidized jobs for the marginally employable. If somehow we could get started placing our first graduates in jobs around the state, I hoped they would do well enough that word of mouth among employers would make it increasingly easy to find work for their successors.

At any event that problem was still a way down the road. First we had to get started. The Godfrey M. Hyams Trust donated $25,000 seed money, and the Van Alan Clark family bought us a dormitory building in Woods Hole. Falmouth area employers rallied behind the effort with offers of apprenticeships in cooking, auto mechanics, small-engine repair, printing, boat building, marine-engine repair, house carpentry, cabinet work, sales, masonry, landscaping, electrical work, plumbing, farm work, laboratory assistance and auto-body repair, among other things. So before the program had even begun, we found ourselves with a range of training opportunities probably unequaled by any similar outfit in Massachusetts.

Not surprisingly the only trouble we ran into came from the public sector. I wanted to avoid the kind of purchase-of-service funding that by tying income to enrollment would pressure us into bringing marginal candidates ashore, so I decided to go after some of the Law Enforcement Assistance Agency money that was being doled out by a group called the Massachusetts Committee on Criminal Justice (MCCJ).

MCCJ's administrator, Gregg Torres, affected the incongruous combination of a pigtail and a three-piece suit. His committee rejected our proposal on the grounds that LEAA guidelines prohibited funding existing organizations. We successfully appealed this decision, thanks largely to the intervention of DYS Commissioner Jack Calhoun, but in the process we offended Mr. Torres, who retaliated by putting every obstacle he could dream up between us and the $52,000 we had been granted. If, he argued, ours was a new program, as we claimed, then it must exist as an entirely separate entity from Penikese, and we could not make completion of the island's program a condition for admission to the mainland.

We countered with the argument that the two programs were mutually reinforcing. Screening our mainland candidates before bringing them ashore would help eliminate the community opposition that had crippled so many programs on which MCCJ's money had already been spent. Besides, we owed it to our participating employers to make sure a boy knew how to work and could be trusted before we asked one of them to take him on. Finally, we thought it was equally imperative that our students themselves see the training program as a continuation of something they had already begun, staffed by people they knew and trusted, rather than as just another program DYS was hassling them with.

This not so tactfully presented rebuttal seemed to get us nowhere. Nonetheless we decided while awaiting the outcome of our negotiations with MCCJ to start up with the Hyams money and hope for the best. Kevin Creedan, a former Columbia University football player who aspired to be a poet, and Eva Reed, who was an occupational therapist, signed on as mainland staff and began doing shifts on the island to get to know the boys they would be working with ashore. The LEAA money was finally released the following April, and shortly afterward our newly named Job Training Center's first three students took up residence in Woods Hole.

We had not yet moved into our new dormitory, so we set up headquarters on a thirty-foot boat a friend had donated to the school and which we moored at my dock in Woods Hole. The island's first students had lived on a boat. It seemed somehow appropriate that the Job Training Center's first students should do the same.

16

THE BLUE CAR with the Mass Official plates that pulled up on the pier one spring day in 1977 was driven by a beefy Irishman wearing a too-tight double-knit jacket. Beside him sat a younger man, and in the back lounged a long-haired boy yawning mightily. The inside handles had been taken off the back doors so the boy could not get out.

Dick Phillips, the driver, saw me and waved. We were friends. Over coffee on his many previous deliveries to Woods Hole he had told me how he nearly made it as a major-league umpire before becoming a staffer at the old Lyman Training School. The reformers had relegated him to "Transportation."

The younger man was a caseworker whom I hadn't met. He opened the back door while Dick unlocked the trunk to fetch our new student's clothes. The boy climbed out and lit a cigarette. "Watch out for this kid," whispered Dick as he handed me the boy's duffle bag.

I introduced myself to the caseworker. He grabbed my thumb in the counterculture handshake, which I fumbled, and there followed an awkward second. "That's Donny," the caseworker said, nodding toward the boy. "Hey, Donny! This guy is George who's gonna drive you down to the island."

"Hi, Donny," I said. "You all set?"

"Yeah, I guess."

"Nervous?"

"Nah!"

"I would be. I hate going places where I don't know anyone."

"I already been sent plenty o' places."

"Yes, I guess you have. Well, if things go well for you on Penikese this should be the last place you ever get sent."

The caseworker reminded me who was calling the shots. "I told Donny if he plays it cool with you guys I can get him a job and his own apartment. Right, Donny?"

Donny seemed unimpressed. "That's what you told me last place I got sent."

"I said if you finished there. You didn't finish. You ran on me."

"Yeah, that place sucked. They was always on my case. That's why I ran."

"You won't have to run from here," I explained. "If you want off, just say so, and I'll come get you. We don't want you to stay if you don't want to be here. OK?"

"Yeah."

The caseworker put his arm around Donny's shoulders. "Blow outta this place, Donny," he warned, "an' they're gonna want to lock you up. I mean, I'm on your side, kid, but you gotta help me. I can't protect you if you don't help me. Right?"

Donny didn't answer.

"Well," I said, "we better get going. Anything else the three of us should talk about?"

"No," said the caseworker. "You got all his papers already. If he gives you any trouble, let me know, an' I'll talk to him myself. Donny and me go way back. He trusts me. Right, kid?"

"Fuckin' asshole," muttered Donny as he climbed on the boat.

There was a north wind that day, so I decided we'd go down the sound instead of the bay. "You want to drive?" I asked Donny as we came around Nonamesset.

"Nah." He sat down and tried to look bored, but a twitching eyelid gave him away.

Maybe if I could get him talking he would forget his fears. "That's Martha's Vineyard over there on the left," I pointed out. "Lots of movie stars live over there."

"Yeah? Who?"

"Oh, lots of them." I tried frantically to think of a name but could only come up with Walter Cronkite.

"Who the fuck is he?"

I guess I'd struck out there. "How about James Taylor? You must have heard of him? The singer? He's got a pet pig—same kind of pig as we've got on the island."

Donny looked at me with an expression of infinite disgust. Then he pretended to go to sleep.

That was fine with me. This run had become so much second nature to me by then that I could use the time to daydream. I thought about Donny's caseworker—long hair, sandals, dungarees, the whole bit—there weren't many of that kind left any more. Idealism was dying at DYS. Jerome Miller's burnt-out reformers were being replaced by more pragmatic types who just happened to find work with the department instead of in some other branch of state government. Donny's caseworker was a throwback to more utopian times. If I read him right, he was the kind who brought enough dedication to his job to try to become personally involved with the boys assigned to him. He believed he could make a difference in their lives. He probably wouldn't last long. For the sake of his own job satisfaction, or self-esteem, or vanity, Donny's caseworker plainly needed to feel needed by Donny, and Donny was going to kick him in the teeth.

My staff ran the same risk. How do you walk the tightrope between emotional involvement and objectivity? There has to be mutual trust for the relationship between a boy and an adult to be effective. Establishing that trust requires an emotional commitment from both of them, and emotional commitments can play havoc with the boy's behavior and the adult's judgment. The problem is that a boy who has known only rejection does not know how to respond to friendship. He may lash out against it, or he may use the other person's concern as a means to manipulate him. Miller's crusaders were all bailing out because they felt themselves betrayed by the kids in whom they had invested so much of themselves.

It looked to me like Donny's caseworker was setting himself up for just such a betrayal. By staking his own self-image on his boy's success he was making himself easy prey to self-delusion. He imagined trust where none existed. His perception of Donny's dependence on him made him possessive. Donny was his triumph. He saw himself as the one who had broken through the boy's hostility, and Donny's trust in him would mean less to the extent that he had to share it with others. His attempt at one-upmanship on the pier grew out of his resentment of me as a potential usurper of his place in Donny's eyes. By painting the world in terms of "them against us," with his role being to protect Donny from others in the system, he was just trying to hold on to the kid. The irony in all this was that in his concern for Donny, he was muddying the water with his own emotional involvement. A less involved pragmatist would have kept things simple: "There it is kid. Take it or leave it."

We were passing Robinson's Hole when it occurred to me with a jolt that I was making many of the same mistakes as Donny's caseworker. I also had tied my success to the success of my students and, by that measure, I was not doing any too well. With four years already invested in the school, the only real achievement I could lay claim to was that we were still in business. David wryly reassured me that at least we were not doing any harm. He was right about that. Instinct more than hard evidence told me that just about all of our students left the island in some small way the better for the experience. We might even have "saved" a couple, although even in those cases the extent of our influence on their salvation was anybody's guess. But for most of our graduates I knew it was wishful thinking to believe that what I had given them was going to have any dramatic impact on their futures.

We were coming up on Penikese.

"Hey, Donny, wake up. We're almost there." Donny stood up, yawning elaborately in case I had any doubts about his nonchalance. John McRoberts was waiting for us on the jetty. I put Donny ashore, wished him good luck, and headed for home.

Job training, I decided while steaming up the bay, was going to be the key to the school's and my own success or failure. The three kids we had brought in to start that program were all, on the basis of their records, "heavy hitters." Gregg Torres certainly couldn't accuse us of limiting enrollment to easy kids, because Barry, Willy and Jonesy were exactly the kind of hard cases whose behavior in other community-based programs was destroying the credibility of the entire reform movement. One success out of this bunch might be attributed to luck. Two would be better, but still not conclusive. If all three made it, then even Mr. Torres would have to admit that the combination of island and job training had done something remarkable. We might, with a few more successes like those three, even be able to claim we had found the cure for delinquency.

I tied up the boat and walked home.

17

—————

BARRY WAS THE SON of a veteran whose disability left him with nothing to do but sit at home and enforce his rigidly old-fashioned rules of behavior. Whenever any one of his seven sons fell short of the mark, the penalty was a home-administered crew cut which left the victim the laughing stock of his long-haired friends. At age twelve Barry ran away to escape the shears, and from that point on his evolution as a delinquent was textbook. First his excellent grades in school went to hell, and he became a habitual truant. Then came "malicious destruction of property," then petty larceny, then car theft and finally armed robbery with a shotgun. This last charge was peculiar in that his alleged victim was later booked as an accomplice, but there was no denying the shotgun. DYS had no choice but to send Barry away. His first stop before coming to us was at DYS's Homeward Bound program, where he impressed the staff with his "perennial grin."

Willy's father boasted lyrically of the many men who had "fallen to his fists," and his son wanted to be just like him. Young Willy was strong and quick, with a huge Afro, and he soon became the terror of the housing projects where he lived. At school he showed exceptional aptitude in art and arithmetic but proved so disruptive in reading class that he repeated second grade three times before anyone thought to test him for dyslexia. Then Willy's mother was killed, and he spent four years in an orphanage until his father remarried. He got along with his stepmother but by that time was already well into his career in crime. By age sixteen he had progressed from stealing toys from department stores to "larceny over $100" and drunken assaults. His friends admired his success with older women and were afraid of his terrible temper.

Jonesy's family lived on the edge of a tidal marsh. Their falling-down shack was guarded by snarling, emaciated dogs. Rusting cars, derelict boats and discarded appliances littered the yard. The inside of the house was such a shambles that it came as all the more a surprise to find Mr. and Mrs. Jones pleasant and well spoken. They would explain to the myriad social workers who came to their door how a conspiracy of events had brought them low. The VA paid Mr. Jones only a pittance for the war injuries that left him unable to work. An unfeeling employer fired Mrs. Jones for not showing up on days when her children were sick. Schoolmates laughed at her boy's tattered clothes. Welfare workers ignored them. The police harassed them. Nonetheless, said Mrs. Jones, she would not complain. Lord knows, she could name some names in her town if she wanted to, but her family had its pride. Mr. Jones was sustained by the memory of his wartime heroism. Mrs. Jones had her unwavering faith. They would not beg. In time God would repay them for their suffering.

I was taken in by all this, and I was not alone. "There has been some talk of paranoid ideation," wrote a psychiatrist who interviewed the family, "but I see no areas of paranoid thought process." This expert was apparently unaware of Mr. Jones' reputation as a violent drunk. He believed the Jones' version of their problems had a "reality basis," and when I met Jonesy himself I had to agree. The boy's clean-cut appearance, diffident smile and obvious candor just did not square with the rape conviction that had led to his referral to Penikese.

Jonesy stoutly maintained his innocence of that charge. With a rueful grin he told me how he, his friends and the alleged rape victim had been drinking. They had stolen a car. He knew they had done the wrong thing, and he had convinced the others that they should return the car to its owner. So they had set off to do this with Jonesy driving. A cop flagged them down. He panicked and in the ensuing chase wrecked the car. The girl claimed she was raped to avoid charges. Why, he asked sadly, did everyone believe her and not him? Why were so many people against him? I didn't know why. Jonesy really did seem to be a victim of circumstances.

Jonesy, Willy and Barry had all taken to Penikese like ducks to water. They had their bad days like everyone else, but most of the time they had so much fun that we had fun being there with them. The staff's comments on their daily score sheets tell the story:

Jonesy
    Worked until we had to make him stop for dinner
    Fine job building a cold frame
    $1 fine for throwing a firecracker out window
    Good initiative
    Nice to have around
    Built a silverware drawer for the kitchen on his own time

Willy
    Finished reading his first book ever
    Caught a 16 lb. bass
    Great job as tour director for a group of visitors
    Trying real hard in school
    Best mechanic out here

Barry
    Worked hard on the wood pile
    Chronic late riser
    Enjoys being given responsibility
    Carved a life-size King Neptune from a driftwood log
    Always cheerful

I was proud of those three kids and prouder yet of what the island had done for them in the four months they had been there. Their caseworkers were impressed. Jonesy's hometown police chief admitted to possibly having written the boy off too soon, and even Barry's father grudgingly conceded "some improvement" in his son.

Barry, who of the three had spent the most time on the island, was the first to come ashore to start the Job Training Center program. Chronic late rising remained a problem, but I was generally able to root him out of his bunk on the boat in time for him to get breakfast at our house before he went off to work as an apprentice to a local building contractor. At the start Barry's performance earned him mixed reviews. By the standards of his exacting boss he was a fast, sloppy workman, but one who listened to criticism and improved steadily. The turning point for him came when he fell off a twenty-foot roof. He hit with a crash, bounced laughing to his feet, and climbed back up as if nothing had ever happened. After that his boss looked at him in a whole new light.

Jonesy came into the program next. Since his job with a boat builder was not due to start right away, I put him to work painting the boat he and Barry were living aboard. This was the first time I had worked closely with him, and I noticed something that perhaps I should have paid more attention to. Jonesy was a perfectionist whose inexperience with a paintbrush made him incapable of meeting his own standards. As I watched him work I saw his face redden and his features contort in suppressed rage. His whole body began shaking so uncontrollably that he had to put down his brush. For a long second he seemed incapable of breathing. Then the moment passed. He went back to his painting, and I pretended I hadn't noticed.

By the time Willy arrived ashore we had taken possession of the former apartment house on Juniper Point that was to become our Woods Hole headquarters. Eva Reed and Kevin Creedan and the three kids set up housekeeping in one of the building's four apartments. We used the second for an office and rented out the other two to make the onshore house self-supporting.

Eva and Kevin worked alternate days supervising the dormitory. Their job was not easy. The kids needed constant prodding to get up, wash, eat, etc. Without this kind of supervision, all three of them would have gone the same way Randy had before them. Each had his own particular problem. Left to his own devices, Jonesy would overdose on sugar, instant coffee and soda. Although anyone else would get hyper on this diet, its effect on him was to make him sullen and morose. Barry would not wash or brush his teeth unless forced to. Willy had to be coerced into doing his share of kitchen work. "What the fuck, Kevin," he would complain, "you sit on your ass all day while we're out workin', an' you won't even cook us dinner!"

"I got the hardest job of any of you," was Kevin's reply. "I get paid to live with assholes. You want to trade jobs?"

Despite the inevitable bitching, our improbable little community got along pretty well. The kids joined in pickup basketball games at the community center and enrolled in night classes at the high school (with the understanding that the staff cooked on school nights). We had nothing but praise from our neighbors. When an annoying fellow whose wife had been mugged in Falmouth asked me to account for the whereabouts of our kids, I had the satisfaction of telling him that at the time in question they were all at school.

Best of all were the reports we were getting from their employers. Barry was developing into a competent framing carpenter, and Willy was showing his artistic talent as an apprentice auto-body man, but Jonesy was our star. "If you've got any more like him," advised the boat builder he worked for, "send them up. I can't find kids that good anywhere."

On Friday, July 3, 1977, I got back from the island in time to go visit our three apprentices. Barry was building a house in Woods Hole. I found him nailing off plywood sheathing. With a handful of nails in one hand and his big framing hammer in the other he moved along with the effortless rhythm some framers never develop; his left hand swung up with the nail, a tap of the hammer set it, three hard whacks drove it home, and then the dance repeated itself. The steady beat of his hammer echoed back from the houses beyond. There was music in it. Barry didn't notice me, and I didn't interrupt his work.

Willy was next. He was outside skylarking with another kid when I drove into the shop. He saw me and sheepishly picked up his tools. The owner, who was usually a hardass, just grinned. "What the hell," he said. "Day like this, I feel like goofin' off myself. Willy's OK. He does real good on the jobs I give him, but he don't exactly go lookin' for work on his own. He'll learn. Hey, we was all kids once. Right?"

The yard where Jonesy worked specialized in restoring classic wooden boats. I got there in time to find Jonesy and Bob Williams, a boat builder friend of mine, bending the last new frame into an ancient Herreshoff. They were having trouble getting the still-steaming oak into place.

"I told him we shoulda yanked the covering boards an' run it in from the top," grinned Jonesy, "but he won't listen. Goddamn guy thinks he knows everything."

"Just shut up an' push where I showed you to push," grunted Bob. "I do know everything."

Jonesy pushed. Bob tapped the heel of the frame across the keel to drive it up under the clamp, and it popped neatly into place.

"See?" said Bob.

"Shit," said Jonesy.

The two of them riveted home the frame with Bob peening and Jonesy bucking. It looked like they had been working together for years.

On the way back Jonesy told me about some work he was doing on a great hulk of a motorboat that sat incongruously among the thoroughbreds in the yard. "Yeah," he said, "She's a real pig. Dunno why the boss took her on. I guess the owner's a friend o' his or somethin'." He shook his head. "I hate workin' on that fuckin' thing. She just ain't our kinda boat."

I laughed out loud. Here was Jonesy, our incorrigible delinquent, becoming a connoisseur of classic boats. Next thing you knew, he'd be in the New York Yacht Club.

When we got to Woods Hole the other two kids were already ready to leave for the weekend. Kevin was waiting to drive them home.

"Come on, Jonesy!" hollered Willy. "Move your ass. My girl can't wait no longer. I gotta go home."

"No way I'm leavin' without a shower," laughed Jonesy. "My girl's waitin' too, an' I ain't about to show up to her place smellin' like Barry."

"Fuck you," said Barry. "That's how the chicks know I'm back in town. They smell me comin', an' they go apeshit."

I left them arguing.

About one o'clock on Saturday afternoon I got a call from Big Willy asking if I had seen his son. Willy had not come home after a party on Friday night. The Taunton Police had just been by looking for him. Apparently a boy had been killed in a car accident, and Willy had been seen earlier in the evening with the victim.

Christ!

I called the Taunton Police. The accident had occurred at 2:15 that morning. The car was a stolen yellow Maverick, and the dead boy had been found in the back seat. His name was Joe Cardoza. "I dunno how the rest of 'em got out," said the desk sergeant. "Whole damn car was wrapped right around the phone pole." There were bloody fingerprints but no other clues. A woman had heard the crash and reported finding a long-haired boy "curled up in a stupor" on her front porch. She had shaken him awake, and he identified himself only as Barry. By the time the police arrived the boy was gone.

I told the sergeant I had a pretty good idea who Barry was and that I would call him back. Then I called Barry's house. Willy answered the phone.

"Willy? What are you doing there? What the hell happened?"

"We was at this party, see? Jonesy an' me, we got in a fight over this broad. He was drunk, man! Actin' real weird. So I split."

"Then what did you do?"

"Nuthin' much. Just walked around some 'til I come to Barry's house. Weren't no lights on, so I slept on the grass."

"Where's Barry? Is he there?"

"Yeah, he's sleepin'. I'll get him for ya."

Barry came to the phone. He sounded scared. "I dunno nuthin', man! No, I weren't in no car. Dunno what you're talkin' about, OK?" He hung up.

I called Willy's parents back to tell them their son was OK. His stepmother told me that around midnight Jonesy and Barry had come by looking for Willy. They were driving a yellow Maverick. There had been another boy in the car.

As soon as I hung up the phone rang again. It was Barry's mother. Barry had admitted to her that he and Jonesy had stolen the car. Jonesy had been driving at the time of the accident. Barry thought Jonesy was hurt. His parents were taking him down to turn himself in to the police.

I passed all this information back to the Taunton desk sergeant and then did the same with Jonesy's hometown police. The chief whom I had earlier assured of Jonesy's rehabilitation sent a squad car over to the Jones place and called me back to report that Jonesy had been home but had left again. There was blood in the kitchen. The investigating officer thought the parents were hiding their injured son.

Jonesy surfaced the next day when he turned up at the Taunton Hospital. He was badly cut up but otherwise not seriously hurt. Barry ended up in the Brockton Hospital with a stiff neck. Both were charged as adults with larceny of a motor vehicle, and Jonesy got homicide on top of that.

Willy did not show up for work the following Monday. His caseworker brought him to Woods Hole on Wednesday, but the boy who came back was not the same one who had left only five days before. "Fuck you guys," he told us. "I don't need this goddamn place."

"The place needs you, Willy," I told him. "You're the only one we have left in Job Training. If you quit now, we're likely to lose the whole show. What about Eva and Kevin? They've put a lot into this. What about the other kids who want the same chance you got? Are you going to let them all down?"

"Fuck 'em," said Willy. "Far as I care they can take your fuckin' Job Training an' shove it up their asses."

So ended his seven months at the Penikese Island School.

I went up to see Barry and Jonesy, who were both still hospitalized. Barry in his neck collar was his usual happy-go-lucky self. His biggest problem, to hear him tell it, was that the damn nurse wouldn't give him a second pillow. Also, the food sucked. I knew him well enough by then not to be entirely fooled by his nonchalance. Still I was taken aback at his complete lack of visible sorrow or remorse. The dead boy, as it turned out, had been one of his best friends. He himself was in deep trouble. With one suspended adult conviction for stolen cars already on his record, he faced almost certain "time" for this new charge. My God, I thought, if he's aware of all this and not showing it, he's one hell of a good actor. It did not seem the right moment to ream him out, however, so I swallowed my disgust and left.

Jonesy was a different story. When I walked into his room he broke down.

"Goddamnit," he wept. "I killed the kid, George. I killed him. What am I gonna do? What am I gonna tell his mom an' dad? Oh, Jesus! Why couldn't it have been me instead?"

I didn't know what to tell him. "He's dead, Jonesy. You have to live with that. But maybe he won't have died for nothing if what you did convinces you to salvage your own life. He wouldn't be dead if you hadn't been drunk. Your father wouldn't be where he is either if he wasn't an alcoholic. You know that, Jonesy. It's probably too late for your father, but it's not too late for you. I think you owe it to that kid never again to take another drink."

He looked up. "You're right," he said quietly.

All the rest of the staff also went up to see Barry and Jonesy, and everybody came back upset at Barry's flippancy and moved by Jonesy's despair. Opinion was divided about whether we should take them back to Penikese while they were awaiting trial. On the one hand we had a rule that anyone picking up new charges was automatically expelled. On the other was the fact that the island had been as close to a decent home as either one of them had ever had. They were both hurt, even if Barry didn't show it, and now was no time to abandon them. We decided to take them back.

It was the wrong decision. Less than a week after their return we caught them both smoking dope. That was it for Barry. He had first come to Penikese over a year before, in March of 1976. We graduated him three months later, and he had asked to come back the following October after picking up new charges in adult court. Now the same pattern had repeated itself. He did brilliantly under supervision and went promptly to hell on his own. There seemed nothing left we could do for him by keeping him at Penikese except perhaps to further postpone the inevitable, so we let him go. Barry had a superb caseworker named Susan Small, who fought successfully to keep him from going to jail. Instead he was sent to a "concept" program which attempted a sophisticated version of the same kind of behavior modification used at Parris Island. The idea was to break a boy down to nothing and then rebuild him in a more positive way, but instead of drill sergeants this program used clinicians, and instead of pushups it used encounter groups.

Barry wrote me a couple of letters while he was in lockup waiting to begin this transformation. As always he was cheerfully optimistic. His new program "sounds really disciplined and hard" but he expected it would "make me think about things," because "a lot of times I do something and not even think about why I did it or what will happen." He hoped they would let him build a model. "I'd like to build the *Constitution* or maybe a motorcycle." That was the last I heard from him.

A year later we learned Barry was in the hospital suffering from suicidal depressions which meant, I suppose, that the clinicians had been able to crack the goofy facade he used so successfully as a shield against his unhappiness. What good that did him, I don't know. Thinking back over the time I knew Barry, I remembered only once seeing a chink in his flippant veneer. That was when he returned from a weekend on which his father had promised to take him fishing.

"How'd it go?" I asked. "Catch anything?"

"Well," he said wistfully, "I dug worms, but we didn't go. Dad was watchin' the ballgame."

Jonesy got another reprieve, mainly because we could not forget his anguish in the hospital. He at least would admit to his problems, and because of that we still thought he had a chance. By then we recognized him for his mother's son. We knew he could be just as plausible, just as skillful at eliciting pity, just as much of a con artist. We also knew he could be just as violent as his father. Despite all that we still responded to something in him that was good. We had seen the Mr. Hyde in Jonesy, but we had also seen the Dr. Jekyll. Although he was plainly a far more dangerous individual than Barry would ever be, Jonesy somehow seemed the more salvageable of the two. Perhaps it was because we sensed that Barry had already given up on himself and Jonesy hadn't. "The thing I have to change," he told us, "is my way of partying and my way of getting angry when there are things I don't understand. If I can do that, I think I can make it." He was sincere.

Almost a year was to pass before Jonesy's case came to trial in the spring of 1978. As the memory of what he had done grew dimmer, he began to forget the resolve he had made in the hospital to take responsibility for his friend's death. On the advice of his lawyer he decided to plead not guilty to homicide and attempt to shift the blame to Barry. He enjoyed the prestige that his long record and the fact that he faced "hard time" gave him with our younger students. As to Joe Cardoza, his death was, according to Jonesy, "his own tough luck. I didn't make him get in the goddamn car."

When I heard that I lost my head. "You sonofabitch," I raged, "you're worse than those goddamn sick bikeys in those magazines you buy. You're so fucked up you're proud of yourself for being an asshole! You think you're some kind of hero because you raped a girl and killed that kid? You call that being a man? Get the hell out of here, you sorry bastard! Go get all your goddamn *Easy Rider* magazines, and look at the pictures of those pot-bellied punks, and then come back and tell me if they're the kind of person you want to be."

Instead he wrote me a letter:

Dear George,

I would like to be a good man, a fair man, a man who cares for others, to be trusted, a hard worker, a damn good boat builder, a good family man, a fun guy to be with, to keep in good shape and I want to have some good sailing adventures and be free and happy and stand on my own two feet and try to be a better man every day.

I'm sorry,

Jonesy

So there was still hope. After he'd been a month on Penikese we brought Jonesy back to Job Training, and he resumed his apprenticeship at the boatyard. His lawyer had apparently decided on delaying tactics in the hope that by the time his client came to trial, Jonesy would have stayed out of trouble long enough to convince the judge to go easy on him. Four times we drove up to the Taunton Court House, and four times the case was continued. On one of these trips, Jonesy, his father and I went outside to get some fresh air on the courthouse steps. Directly across the street the Taunton Police Station was undergoing renovations. A wall was torn out, and we could look right into the second floor to see the cells.

"See the one in the middle?" asked Jonesy's father. "I been in that one. Yessir," he said with obvious pride, "it took five pigs to get me inside, an' there weren't one of them wasn't bleedin', time they were done. You can bet your old man kicked some ass that night! You better believe I did."

"Are you proud of that?" I asked, but before he could answer we had to go back inside.

Jonesy's lawyer tried next to have the case thrown out on grounds that his client had been denied a speedy trial. That didn't work, so on May 4, 1978, we went up to Taunton for the last time. My record of the day reads:

> Jonesy pleaded not guilty on all charges and therefore had to sit through a long trial in which the state conclusively proved its case against him. . . . Although he was probably too nervous to follow everything that went on, the experience must have made some impact on him. He shares his family's ability to convince himself that he is always the innocent victim of circumstance, but after hearing gruesome clinical descriptions of the cause of death, I doubt if even he could still lay the blame for what happened on drugs, on Barry or on anyone else but himself.

Jonesy was found guilty on all charges and given two concurrent eighteen-month sentences which were suspended for two years on condition that he satisfactorily complete another year in our job-training program. Judge, lawyer and probation officer all assured him that he was a very lucky man.

The rest of the story is quickly told. No longer faced with the prospect of jail, Jonesy immediately went to hell. He began again to drink heavily on his weekends at home and to use marijuana in Woods Hole. The court made one last effort to avoid executing his sentence by giving him ten days in the Barnstable House of Correction for parole violation in the hope that seeing jail firsthand might convince him to change his ways. Shortly after his release from Barnstable, he was arrested for driving without a license, and while awaiting trial on that charge, he was picked up once again for forcing his way into a girl's apartment at knife point. In both cases he had been drunk. So it ended up that our efforts to keep

Jonesy out of jail ultimately resulted in his being sent away with two new charges on top of his original ones.

We had done him a disservice by continuing to insulate him from the consequences of his behavior. His entire experience with the Department of Youth Services, with us, and ultimately with his first exposure to the adult court system served to convince him that no matter what he did wrong, there would always be people willing to give him a break as long as he was sincerely sorry for what he had done. When, as was inevitable, he finally pushed the system too far, he went to jail believing that he was being sent only because the same people who had helped him in the past had suddenly turned around and betrayed him. Jonesy saw himself as the perpetual victim, with DYS, the courts, Penikese Island and even the victims of his crimes all linked in some inexplicable conspiracy to destroy him.

18

OUR JOB TRAINING CENTER, meanwhile, was staggering back onto its feet. As enrollment crept back up to our maximum of five students, I realized what an awful job we had saddled on Eva and Kevin. Work on the island had a certain amount of glamour. There the staff operated as a mutually supporting team of three or four adults. Each one had a particular interest—boats, garden, shop, kitchen, etc.—in which he or she could find refuge no matter how unpleasant the day might otherwise be. The island staff were with the kids at the worst of times but also at the best of times, and they were backed up by the powerful magic of Penikese itself. When their shift was over, they could look forward to the traditional stop at the Leeside Bar in Woods Hole, where they unwound telling stories over pitchers of beer.

Eva and Kevin had none of that. They worked alone, and they felt very much second-class citizens to their counterparts on Penikese. They only saw students when the kids were at their very worst. In the mornings the boys were surly. In the evenings they were bored. The better they did at their jobs, the worse they behaved in the dormitory. "It's as if they've got a certain amount of shit they need to get out of their systems every day," said Kevin, "and if it doesn't come out at work, we get it all here."

The Job Training staff's problems were compounded by pressure to maintain a high enough enrollment to keep the MCCJ administrator off our backs. As a result we brought some pretty marginal candidates ashore. Woods Hole was a pretty Bohemian place, but even so our kids stood out like sore thumbs. Watching them swaggering through town reminded me how much we were expecting them to change their lifestyles. The haircuts, mannerisms, speech and dress which branded them as punks were the accepted standards of the only part of the world where they felt they had a place. Those same affectations often disguised their educational and cultural deficiencies. The kids who laced their conversation with "fuck" were generally using this ubiquitous word to plug the gaps in their vocabularies. Perhaps part of our troubles at Job Training arose from pushing them to abandon the trappings of their world before they had the confidence to believe they could adopt the trappings of ours.

Whatever the reason the results of Job Training's first year were awful. Seven of our eleven students had to be returned to DYS for poor performance or new charges. Our one graduate was re-arrested within a week of going home. Only three kids were still in the program. Eva and Kevin had just about had it.

So had I. I was sick of bureaucrats and sicker of delinquents. Worst of all I no longer trusted my own instincts. I had fancied myself a realist in this business. I had written condescendingly of the bleeding-heart reformers, and yet while I had been assuring skeptics that they had nothing to fear from Willy, Barry and Jonesy, those three had been going home to steal cars and do God knows what else on their weekends. When we moved the kids ashore we faced the same problems as every other community-based program, and we had done no better than the rest of them. If results were the measure, my Job Training Center was just another mediocre member in the undistinguished fraternity of private rehabilitation contractors.

So I was in a gloomy frame of mind as I headed down the bay to spend the day on Penikese. I arrived just ahead of Bishop Loring, who came steaming into the cove just after I'd tied up. He rowed into the beach, where I met him.

"Hello! Hello!" said the Bishop, climbing stiffly out of his skiff. "Came by myself today. Mrs. Loring's under the weather, but she sent some cookies. Damn it, left 'em on the boat. Have to go back for 'em. Can't remember anything any more."

He asked for news of the school. I told him of Job Training's dismal record and said I was about ready to pack it up. "Well, you can't," said the Bishop with a trace of irritation. "*He* meant you to do this work, and you musn't let *Him* down."

I watched with increasing anxiety that afternoon as the wind picked up from the east, but the Bishop as usual remained oblivious to the weather and paid no attention to my suggestions that he'd better get home ahead of the coming storm. By evening, when I walked him back down to the dock, it was blowing so hard that just getting in his anchor would have been a hard job even for a much younger man. He would accept no help, however, and rowed out alone through the chop to his pitching boat. I watched him crawl unsteadily out onto his foredeck, and I thought to myself that if that frail old man could heave up his anchor in those conditions then I sure as hell ought to be able to hang on with Penikese. The Bishop hauled it aboard and roared away, forgetting as always to lower his outdrive.

Bishop Loring died not long afterward, but St. Aiden's Chapel in South Dartmouth continues to support the school in his memory. This seems to me more fitting than that parish perhaps realizes, since were it not for the Bishop that stormy evening, there probably would have been no school left to support.

More troubles were still to come, thanks once again to Jonesy.

During his time on Penikese following his conviction, Jonesy came under the supervision of the Bristol County Probation Department. Since he remained committed to DYS, he was at the same time answerable to his caseworker. Penikese and his parents also figured in the picture, and it was never very clear who was responsible for what. This situation was an ideal one for the Joneses, since their considerable talent for manipulating the system lay in their ability to play the various people involved one against the other.

The principal players in the resulting drama were a study in contrasts. Ted Chadwick and Bill McAndrew, the chief and assistant chief probation officers for the Bristol County First District Court, were two very professional law-enforcement officials. With cynical good humor and inadequate resources they went about trying to salvage what they could in a fundamentally lost cause. They believed in rehabilitation but didn't forget their responsibility to protect society. Facts, not feelings, dictated their decisions. If a convict met the terms of his probation, well and good. If he didn't, he went back to jail. Their job got more complicated when the jails were full, which was just about always. Then they had to factor in the severity of a man's charges, the nature of his parole violation, and their instinctive feeling for how great a menace he posed to society, in order to decide how best to handle him without further undermining the credibility of the criminal-justice system. It was quite a balancing act. Neither Ted nor Bill had any illusions about Jonesy from the first moment they saw him. Plausible criminals were their stock in trade.

Jonesy's DYS caseworker, a Mr. Bailey, was a decent fellow but entirely unsuited to his job. More than most, he needed to believe he was in the driver's seat. Jonesy, however, now belonged to Ted Chadwick, and DYS was left in the unhappy position of paying the bills without calling the shots. We continued to send the department monthly progress reports along with our invoices, but we were in much more frequent communication with Ted and Bill. The two of them often came down to visit Jonesy at the boatyard, and they followed his declining performance closely enough not to be surprised when we recommended that he be locked up for ten days after we caught him again smoking dope.

Bailey, on the other hand, was openly horrified at our callousness and saw in what we had done the chance to reassert his influence with his boy. Before talking with us he told Jonesy that in his opinion we had seriously overreacted to a very trivial offense. Jonesy, of course, played the poor guy like a fiddle. With the same expression of injured bafflement he had once used so effectively on me, the boy told Bailey that he was being punished because of some inexplicable vendetta Eva and Kevin had against him. Yes, there had been a little dope. He was sorry about that, and he wouldn't make the same mistake again. But he didn't really think dope was the problem. Eva and Kevin just didn't like him. That's why they were sending him away.

Bailey dutifully reported all this back to his superiors at DYS. Jonesy, with the department as his ally, decided to fight the ten-day termination of his parole. Ted Chadwick cheerfully set up a hearing on the case and assured Jonesy and Bailey that he would take the occasion to recommend execution of the full eighteen-month sentence. Faced with that possibility Jonesy elected ten days instead. He spent his time behind bars, convinced as always that he was the innocent victim. The idea that the experience was intended to prevent him from spending a lifetime locked up was as lost on him, as it was evidently on DYS. Two weeks after his release from Barnstable, he was back in jail facing the "hard time" he liked to boast about on Penikese.

At the time Jonesy's sad story was playing itself out, we were negotiating a new purchase-of-service contract with DYS. Ray Mason, Jim McGinnes' successor as director of Region VII, was not one of my fans. He used the pretext of our disagreement over Jonesy to hold up action on our rate increase and suggested that the differences in philosophy between Penikese and DYS were perhaps irreconcilable.

That did it. I guess ever since that afternoon with the Bishop I had been subconsciously looking for a way to get clear of Penikese without feeling like a quitter. Ray Mason gave me an excuse to do just that. I fired off an intemperate letter to him demanding a written critique of our philosophy and of our handling of Jonesy. After two months had gone by without an answer to my letter or any action on our new contract, I had my way out. On September 1, 1978, I wrote the group of friends and supporters we had elected to our Penikese Island Corporation recommending that if our differences with DYS could not be resolved within fifteen days we should close the school or else find some other purpose for it.

When news of this ultimatum reached Boston, DYS Commissioner Jack Calhoun came down to Penikese to find out what was going on. He and his two assistant commissioners, John Isaacson and Jim Wells, arrived on a fine October afternoon. It was too nice a day to be inside, so we gathered on the hill above the house to discuss whether or not the program we offered at Penikese was compatible with the department's approach to rehabilitation. Jack was as good at getting right to the point as I was at rambling off on a tangent. I was discoursing on the importance of teaching accountability when he cut me off by asking, "What do you need to do the job right?"

"If we're right in emphasizing accountability," I replied, "what we need more than anything else is for you guys to back us up. To teach boys to connect actions to consequences, we've got to function as part of a system that has teeth in it. We need to set up a sequence of increasingly severe responses to repeat offenders."

"OK," said Jack. "We can give you that. You and John can work out the details. What else?"

"Staff!" I said. "The reason your contractors aren't any better is because their staff burn out even before they've learned enough to be really effective. This job is more demanding than public-school teaching, and yet the pay is less and the hours longer. You get what you pay for, it's as simple as that."

"Is pay the problem, or is it hours?"

"Both, but if I had to choose I'd say most people run out of energy before they run out of money. If we're really going to improve the system, I think we've got to make it possible for people to consider making this kind of work a career in the same way that people make teaching a career. We can't rely forever on idealistic kids who are going to go like hell for six months and then move on to something else."

"You all seem older," observed John Isaacson. "How long have your staff been working at Penikese?"

David Masch answered that one. "Right now the average is just a little over two years, but we've been a lot luckier than most. We've got this island to thank for that and also Woods Hole. People seem to come to Woods Hole looking for this kind of thing. Also just about all of us work at something else during our time off. What we need most to stay sane and to do our other jobs is longer breaks between shifts."

"So what do you think would be the ideal enrollment and staffing pattern for Penikese?" asked Jack.

What the hell, I thought, we might as well shoot for the moon. "Nine kids and three teams of four staff each."

"Whew! You guys don't want much do you? Nine kids and twelve staff! OK, let's try it. How long are the kids going to stay, and also what about Job Training?"

"Well, it seems most kids peak at about four months, but we'd like to give them the option to stay longer if they want to. Every once in a while one does. As to Job Training, not everybody is going to qualify to come ashore. They're going to have to earn that. I'd say we'd average four kids in Job Training, so the two staff we've got now should be enough."

"Fourteen staff plus George and a secretary for thirteen kids just isn't going to fly, Jack," said John. "Can you imagine what it would cost us if that ratio was applied statewide?"

"Well," I butted in defensively, "you asked what it would take to do the job right."

"Yes," said Jack, "I am interested to learn what it would take to do the job right. Let's just think of this as an experiment and play it out. What else would we need for our ideal program?"

"Follow up," shot Jim Wells. "With all those staff you'd be able to stay in touch with your graduates after they returned home. That way if it looked like one was slipping, you might even be able to bring him back for a while."

"Make the numbers look better, too," opined John. "Let's see, if you actively tracked your graduates for, say, six months after they left, you could show twenty-seven kids on your books, which doesn't look bad."

David, however, saw the problems with this. "We could certainly stay in touch, but I don't know how much time we'd have to go running all over the state without burning out, which is what we're trying to avoid. Maybe the way to do it would be when we drove the island kids home for their weekend, we could check in on nearby graduates then."

"A lot of them would need more supervision in their hometowns than that amount of contact would provide," said Jim. "We'd probably have to contract with somebody else to provide it."

"Can't do that," said John, the realist. "With purchase-of-service you can't pay two programs for the same kid."

"If you're talking about the ideal program," I said, "you sure as hell won't want to use a purchase-of-service contract. That method of payment has been responsible for more of your contractors' going belly-up than anything else DYS has done or left undone. It leaves us holding the bag when you guys run out of money. It pressures us to take kids we know we should not accept and to keep kids we should unload. It delays payment while your regions fiddle around processing invoices. It's the sorriest goddamn arrangement—"

"If you're leading up to asking for a fixed-price contract," interrupted John, "forget it, unless you're willing to forfeit the right you keep insisting on to reject what you consider to be unsuitable kids. The only contractors we can pay fixed price are the ones who can provide secure treatment for whoever we send them. If you can give us that, Penikese has a value to the department even when you're below the enrollment we're paying for. That's because we know you'll be there when Boston Court sends us a triple rapist and we need a place to put him."

"Come on, John," I objected, "we've been down this road before. Look around you, for chrissake! You know we can't take any screamer you send us and put him down here with an axe in his hands—"

"OK, then, but don't try to have it both ways. You're right: purchase-of-service does force you to keep up your enrollment. That's the way we planned it. If we paid all you guys fixed price and let you pick the kids you took, we'd be looking at a lot of half-full programs, and then the legislature would be looking at us."

"That may be true—it probably is—but the only thing I can tell you is that from our end, purchase-of-service just doesn't work. There's got to be some middle ground. Seems to me you wouldn't be going too far out on a limb if you paid fixed price for say, twelve-month contract periods to carefully screened outfits. You wouldn't have to renew their contracts if they didn't prove themselves a good buy. Besides, if you backed us up better with short-term detention for our fuck-ups, you might find we could hang on to a lot of the kids we've now got no choice but to send back to you."

"Well," said Jack, "we won't know that if we don't try it. So along with 'backing you up,' as you put it, you're also asking for a fixed-price contract which is not tied to your enrollment and which is paid out of our central office rather than through the regions?"

"That's exactly what we're asking for."

"OK, you got it."

Now how could I quit? Jack Calhoun was giving us virtually a blank check to do the job right, and I couldn't very well walk out on him after that. Besides, with adequate staff, adequate funding and the department to back us up with the threat of lockup, we might now make the breakthrough that had so far eluded us—and everyone else. It was worth another shot.

But something inside me had changed. I had made the same mistake with Barry and Jonesy as I had predicted that Donny's caseworker would make with Donny. During the weeks that those two boys had lived on the boat by our house they had become part of my family. Barry, the goofball, was a wildly popular older brother to my two sons, while Jonesy and I had gone on a couple of those "sailing adventures" he dreamed about. In the mornings I used to watch the two of them come skylarking up to the house for breakfast and think to myself how far removed those healthy, clear-eyed kids were from the sullen delinquents they had been only a few months before. In the evenings after dinner I enjoyed watching our two former street fighters invent pretexts for sticking around while I read aloud to George and Tommy. The five of us went through the entire *Bounty* Trilogy and spent our mealtimes debating whether Captain Bligh was a villian or a hero. Those were good times.

Barry and Jonesy were among the handful of apparently salvaged lives I could point to as the product of five years of work, and I had used them to beat back my growing doubts about the value of my now no longer new career.in rehabilitation. I was hearing from friends who had been my juniors in the Marine Corps and were already making Lieutenant Colonel, and I found it hard to avoid disparaging comparisons between running a school for eight students and running the battalion I might now be commanding if it hadn't been for that goddamn mine. My doubts were reinforced by increasing disenchantment with the school among some of Leo Cohen's Friends of Penikese. These successful types who for three years had been raising a lot of money for a program they expected to grow into a rehabilitation empire to rival Boy's Town were disappointed by our refusal to get bigger and by our candid pessimism about what we were achieving. Penikese did not conform to a high roller's idea of success, and so gradually the Friends' interests shifted elsewhere. I was no longer certain enough they were wrong not to resent their defection. Consequently I grew to dread the question asked by everyone first learning about the school. "How many boys are at Penikese?" some potential benefactor would inquire, and the raised eyebrows and brief pauses that followed my reply, "Eight," would signal what my disappointed listeners were thinking: "What the hell kind of place is this, with nearly as many teachers as it's got students?"

All my reservations, however, were banished, at least temporarily, whenever I saw Barry and my sons working earnestly together over some model motorcycle, or when I went up to the boatyard to see new evidence of Jonesy's growing skill. At such times as these I would in my imagination ask my more visibly successful friends how many of them could claim to have banished as much unhappiness as I had done.

Then came that car accident and all the evidence which followed to prove that I had done nothing of the sort. That for me was the end of innocence. Since then I have made it a point to keep a little distance between me and the boys who have followed Barry and Jonesy to Penikese.

19

W E NEVER GOT A CHANCE to run the experiment Jack Calhoun had conceived that fall afternoon on Penikese. Governor Dukakis was unseated in the 1978 state Democratic primary,
and for several uneasy months after the elections Jack was neither
reappointed nor replaced by the new Democratic administration.
His friends mounted a letter-writing campaign on his behalf, but
it was to no avail. Even more than most Massachusetts politicians,
Governor Edward King set about surrounding himself with cronies
met during his career on the fringes of politics. Law and order had
been one of the big issues in his campaign. Both in the nation and
in Massachusetts the trend was toward "getting tough on crime."
Jack, the first DYS commissioner since Jerome Miller to publicly
acknowledge the need to lock up dangerous delinquents, was unfairly painted as a "bleeding heart" and relieved. John Isaacson
moved over to head the Office for Children, and Jim Wells left the
department. Their successors at DYS inherited a Penikese contract
whose purpose they did not understand and whose cost they found
excessive.

I don't know whether the problems which followed were due
simply to inertia on the part of people uninterested in making the
contract work or whether we were actively opposed by those who
resented our favored status with Jack. For whatever the reasons,
only one DYS regional director, our old friend John McElligott from
the Western Region, actively supported the program. Although we
met early in the year to explain what we offered to the placement
supervisors from the four regions who had been allocated slots at

Penikese, most of the kids they sent us were brought down by case-workers who knew nothing about Penikese and were not aware of the type of back-up they were contractually committed to provide. When we first requested temporary detention for a boy who had twice pulled a knife, his region's reaction was to complain that a program costing as much as those offering secure treatment was "sending its problems back to the department."

Twenty-nine boys came down for interviews in the course of 1979. Twenty-four were accepted. Two of them ran, three left at their own request, six were kicked out, and thirteen graduated. Even our graduates were primarily time servers. But despite low student motivation and the usual share of misunderstandings with DYS, 1979 was our best year yet. Gone was the temptation, chronic to all understaffed programs, to make keeping the peace a higher priority than demanding acceptable performance. The enlarged staff, averaging thirty-two years of age and three years of experience at Penikese, found itself better able to push students harder to face up to their individual problems. Despite the potential for increased tension inevitable to this effort, the island was a calmer and happier place than ever for both students and instructors. Even Job Training improved, although working there remained so unpleasant that after Eva and Kevin resigned we began rotating the island staff onto the mainland for brief tours "in the barrel." Nobody looked forward to working ashore, but collectively we were able to hold the lid on things, with one dramatic exception involving a boy named Don.

Don had not entirely shed his baby fat when he first came to Penikese, and we had done society no favor by giving him the opportunity to develop into probably the strongest boy we've ever had on the island. By the time he moved ashore he could effortlessly shoulder two 100-pound feed bags and carry them from the pier up the steep hill to the barn a quarter of a mile away. Don idolized the Stallone types he saw on TV who had taught him to measure his manhood by his capacity for violence. Unlike his role models, however, he wasn't acting.

We were uneasy about bringing him in to Job Training, but the program needed students, and we succumbed to the pressure to keep enrollment high enough to satisfy Gregg Torres, our critical administrator from the Massachusetts Committee on Criminal Justice. Don's apprenticeship was with a sand-and-gravel company where he spent his days moving huge concrete castings and learning to operate heavy equipment. He was a good worker but a scary presence, especially to the young bookkeeper who often worked alone in the remote trailer that served as the company office.

Don's performance in the dormitory was marginal, so that when he was picked up at home one weekend for breaking and entering, it didn't take us long to decide to expel him. Two days later he and a carload of drunken punks showed up in Woods Hole, allegedly to pick up his clothes. We threw them out, and Don departed, boasting that he was going back to the sand-and-gravel plant to "rip off" his old boss. So we alerted the police, who arrested Don in Falmouth that evening for trying to cash checks he had stolen from us. Before he was picked up, he went by the house of a former coworker. This man's wife and small children were home alone, so Don and his friends spent the afternoon drinking beer, shouting obscenely and pissing all over the porch while the young mother and her daughters cowered inside the house. The merchant who had cashed the checks and the coworker's wife were very decent about the whole thing, but we all felt pretty awful about the trouble we had brought to Falmouth.

Incidents such as that one showed we were still far from perfect, but all in all we did a creditable job of holding up our end of the deal we had made with Jack Calhoun. We put together what I think was unquestionably the most qualified group of instructors ever to staff a DYS program. Every one of them was exceptional; together they were superb. If one of Jack's goals had been to attract qualified people to this field, we certainly gave him that.

The question we couldn't answer was whether our improved school was producing improved graduates. To find out we decided to run a follow-up study on the 106 boys who attended Penikese between 1973 and 1978 and use this data as a basis for comparison with the records of graduates from our current program, now adequately funded thanks to Jack Calhoun's intervention.

A salty old juvenile-probation officer whose opinion I respected threw up his hands in disgust at this idea. "You goddamn crusaders," he growled, "I don't need no study to tell me what I already know. You gotta understand by now that no matter what we do, we're going to lose at lot more than we win. If you guys go around publishing the figures showin' how bad we do, then the public and the legislature and everyone else will just throw in the towel, and we'll end up losing even the few kids we are able to save."

He had a point, but I thought the same argument also cut the other way. If the "public and the legislature and everyone else" could be made to face up to how many delinquents were passing un-changed through our rehabilitation system, then perhaps they would be more willing to root out the causes of the disease rather than just continuing to ineffectually treat the symptoms. I knew that in anything short of an Orwellian society not much could be done about the kind of genetically based tendencies Jonesy inherited from his father. But our society could at least face up to the implica-tions of the profoundly confusing American ethic, which glorifies violence when used on the side of "right." We could do more to alleviate the early-childhood nutritional deficiencies that damage minds and bodies. We could cut through the hype and the bigotry and the selfish interest groups that stand in the way of an effective campaign against drugs, drunkenness, and unwanted pregnancies. We might even be able to convince Messrs. Stallone, Eastwood, Schwarzenegger and the rest of those Hollywood jerks to prove their manly prowess by climbing mountains rather than wasting their enemies.

On the other hand, I didn't think the public would ever do any of the things needed to curb delinquency as long as upbeat articles in national magazines about allegedly successful rehabilitation pro-grams made it so easy to believe the problem could be made to go away. If the success rates being claimed in these stories were even close to accurate, those programs were working miracles. Usually, however, a closer reading suggested that the statistics were suspect. Success was claimed but not well defined. If the measure was the number of graduates who didn't reappear in juvenile court, were the kids who turned seventeen and went on to adult prisons successes? How long did a boy have to stay clean to qualify as having made it? Some programs claiming success hadn't been in business long enough to accumulate meaningful statistics. How was their data gathered? The number of our graduates I knew of who had already dropped out of sight made me wonder if compiling valid figures was even possible.

It seemed to me success really had to be measured in positive terms. There were a lot of ruined lives out there that never showed up in court. Any meaningful study would have to limit its claims of success to those who were productively occupied and free of involvement with any public correctional, welfare or mental-health agencies. I suspected that if this standard was applied by the people claiming success, they would find that what they were documenting was at best a remission of symptoms rather than a cure.

In any event, we would find this out for ourselves. Woolcott Smith, the Oceanographic's statistician, agreed to help us set up the study and run it through his computers. Phil Rollins, our district attorney, got us access to the Department of Probation's records in Boston, and Bill McAndrew, Jonesy's old probation officer, showed us how to decode the records themselves. The Godfrey M. Hyams Trust put up the money to pay for the whole thing, and Sue Heywood came in from the island to gather the data.

When all the results were in, we found that the average age of the boys we looked at when they first arrived at Penikese was 16.29. Their average grade level was 8.4, but their actual academic level was half that. The study group had averaged 0.34 arraignments per month from the time of their first arrest until they had come to Penikese. After leaving the school their average dropped to 0.21 month.

Their crimes were classified as "Against Persons" or "Against Property." Before coming to Penikese the study group had amassed 105 charges for crimes against persons and 1,478 charges for crimes against property. After Penikese the ratio of crimes against persons (204) increased significantly relative to crimes against property (1,614).

"Home Situation" was broken down into categories including boys who while at Penikese were living with natural parents (47), a single parent (46), natural parent and stepparent (10) and relatives or foster parents (3).

We used daily scores to rate each boy's "Performance on the Island." We found that 40 did well, 31 average, and 35 poorly. Boys were further divided into categories by their length of stay. Fifteen spent under 30 days on Penikese, 53 were there more than 30 days but for one reason or another failed to graduate, and 38 graduated. Finally we used court records and Sue's assessment of performance since leaving the school to assign each boy to what Woolcott called a "Success Index." The 16 boys designated as "good prospects" were productively occupied, free of the criminal-justice system and optimistic about their futures. The 37 "fair prospects" had little sense of future, sporadic employment and continuing minor brushes with the law, while the 53 "poor prospects" posed serious threats to society and were likely to spend much of their lives behind bars. On the arbitrarily selected date of April 1, 1980, 32 of the last category were actually in jail.

Woolcott's computers juggled all this data around and came up with some interesting correlations: Our sixteen good prospects turned out to have averaged a greater number of arraignments *before* coming to Penikese than either the fair prospects or the poor prospects. A boy's chances for success increased with the amount of time he spent at the school The ratio of charges against persons to charges against property increased dramatically among the poor prospects. Boys with stepparents did worse than boys with single parents. Nothing in the backgrounds of the good prospects served to differentiate them from the other two groups.

We graded the 24 students who came to Penikese in 1979 under the new contract against the same Success Index used in the study for old graduates, even though this was a largely subjective process in view of the short time that had elapsed since the new kids' departures. That group produced 2 good prospects (8.33 percent) 15 fair prospects (62.51 percent), and 7 poor prospects (29.16 percent). These figures looked somewhat better than those from the report (16 percent, 34 percent, 50 percent), but Woolcott assured us we could expect some of the fair prospects to migrate over time in both directions to bring the 1979 statistics more in line with those of previous years. Although our percentage of graduates was 54 percent in 1979, up from 38 percent in 1978, this improvement was probably due more to the expanded staff's better ability to keep boys in line than to any significant improvement in their behavior or long-term prospects.

All in all there was no escaping the conclusion that we had not given Jack Calhoun's successors at DYS a very good return on their money. But if our mandate from DYS was still, as Jack had wanted, to maximize the number of "good prospects" among our graduates, the follow-up study showed us how to do it.

Since a boy's prospects improved proportionately to the time he spent at the school, we decided to make Job Training a mandatory sequel to the island in 1980. (For all their bitching and squealing while they were in the program, the boys who successfully completed Job Training were usually "good prospects.") We would not change our open enrollment policy, because our study had revealed no patterns that would enable us to identify candidates who had better-than-average chances for success. We would, however, be more ruthless in weeding out anyone who showed himself to be too poor a risk to bring ashore.

When the time came to renew our contract with DYS, I took our new proposal to John McElligott, who was then reluctantly serving as acting DYS assistant commissioner in Boston. John was one of our strongest supporters, and I could always count on him for straight answers. He wasted no time telling me that our more "elitist" program would not fly. Penikese was proposing to do more for less kids at a time when the department was geing pressed by the ever-increasing number of delinquents to do less for more.

"Face it, George," John told me, "with the size of our budget and the number of kids the courts are sending us, we're just not going to change that many lives. About all we can hope to do is yank the most out-of-control kids off the street, cool them down a bit in a place like Penikese, and turn them loose again with the hope that a little good rubs off on them somewhere along the way." He went on to explain how growing pressure from the law-and-order faction in the legislature was forcing DYS to tip the scales away from rehabilitation towards protecting the public. How many kids DYS could get off the street for its money had to be at least an equal consideration to the quality of care purchased.

"If that's the case," I asked, "why don't you scrap the community-based experiment and go back to lockups?"

"No, damn it," John said. "For all its problems what we're doing now is a whole lot better than what we did before. The way I see it, if you take a boy who has had nothing but bad experiences, and you give him one good one, you've made him better than what he was. That's what you're doing on Penikese. You're giving kids maybe the only good experience they're ever going to get. But don't think you're going to change the world."

"No, I know that, but I still think you'd do better if you locked up the kids you can't do anything for and sent the others to us. Just trying to cool kids off doesn't contribute a whole lot either to rehabilitation or to protecting the public."

"Are you going to sort them out for us?" John demanded. "You've said yourself you can't tell from a boy's record how he'll do on the island."

"Let them sort themselves out. Give everyone a chance, maybe even several chances, but if a kid keeps on picking up new charges despite our efforts to help him, more of the same kind of help isn't likely to change things. So lock him up and use his space at Penikese or wherever he's at for another, less damaged boy who will get more out of it."

"Have you ever been inside one of our lockups? We have teachers, gyms, shops, psychiatrists, the whole bit, but what we really have is a bunch of the most screwed-up kids in the state all packed in under one roof. Most of them came out of there worse than they went in."

"Maybe," I said, "but if that study we did is representative, most all of the kids I'm talking about locking up will go on to become criminals anyway, so what difference does it make?"

"The difference between us, my friend," said John, "is that you see things as black and white, and I see them as many shades of gray. I don't think it's right to let any kid hang himself because of the things he's done as a teenager. So I'd rather see us keep muddling along as we're doing now than have us write off as lost causes all the kids you would have me lock up."

John and I went back and forth this way without either of us convincing the other. The upshot of it all was that the department agreed to fund the island for one more year. Support for Job Training was dropped on the grounds that boys stable enough to qualify for that program had already received as much help as DYS could afford to give them. We were told that the money to support our apprentices was needed for boys whose immediate situations were more critical.

The loss of Job Training was a major setback, but I must admit to a feeling of relief when the program's last graduate left for the Navy in September 1980. Job Training had on a percentage basis been more successful than the island, but the program had not been an asset to the Woods Hole community. Every time we had some crisis such as the one Don created I had asked myself what right I had to inflict these kids on my neighbors.

John McElligott fled Boston to return to his DYS region and we began another year on Penikese. The contract for FY 1980 cost DYS $225,000 and set the maximum enrollment on the Island at nine. Penikese was to be considered cost effective if our population averaged seven for the year.

As the year wore on it became increasingly clear that we were not giving DYS what it wanted to buy. The department's current priorities favored programs that would essentially warehouse delinquents by providing such low-stress environments that every student would finish his time without running. Our interest remained in working with the kids who could profit most from what we had to offer. We continued to stress accountability, but our requests for back-up from the regions were met with increasing annoyance. Referrals began to fall off. The weather also conspired against us. The winter of 1980-81 produced the worst ice in recent memory. Buzzards Bay froze solid as far west as Quick's Hole. For a while we were able to work our way through the float ice in Vineyard Sound, but by mid-January even the sound was so chocked with ice floes that we could no longer find a channel on either side of the islands. So we left a caretaker on Penikese to feed the animals and moved the whole operation into the now vacant Job Training dormitory. During the month that we remained in

Woods Hole we could not accept even the few new referrals we did receive.

Events in Boston, meanwhile, were working to further compound our problems. The governor appointed a Task Force on Juvenile Crime which lambasted DYS for its overly permissive policies. Among the task force's conclusions were recommendations that the courts be re-empowered to confine delinquents and that juveniles convicted of violent crimes be given mandatory sentences to lockup.

The reform movement was still strong enough to prevent the power to confine juveniles from being restored to the judges, but the price of the victory was agreement to a massive relocation of the department's funds from community-based programs to more secure facilities. Penikese, with an annual cost per student of $25,000, was obviously not going to survive the coming purge.

When our contract expired we were given the option of going back to a purchase-of-service contract, but that semed like a giant step in the wrong direction. We hadn't been able to meet our expenses from public money when we had operated under that arrangement before 1979, and it was no more likely that we would be able to do so now. There seemed no alternative but to close down.

Our last student left the island on June 26, 1981, and the model program that we and Jack Calhoun had pinned our hopes on nearly three years before ended without ever getting a fair test.

20

B Y PULLING OUR CONTRACT DYS was giving me another excuse to get out from under Penikese, and I was powerfully tempted to use it. The terms of our agreement with our landlords at the Division of Fish and Wildlife dictated that if we closed the school we would have to remove all our buildings and equipment from the island. I tentatively offered the whole plant—lock, stock and barrel—to Dick Cronin, who had replaced Jim Shepard as Fish and Wildlife's director, but Dick's budget did not have funds to pay for a caretaker, and his lawyers advised that our abandoned buildings would constitute an "attractive nuisance" which could get the division sued if some trespasser was hurt on the island.

It looked like we would have to tear everything down. So one July day I went down to my now-silent school to see what dismantling it would involve. Our flimsy boathouse behind the pier would be no problem—we'd been planning to get rid of that anyway—but the shop building further up the hill was a different story. John McRoberts and Otto Reber had built that one to last. I went inside, past the half-finished projects the kids had left on the benches when we closed, and looked up at the intricately fitted rafters under Otto's hip roof. A lot of work had gone into those rafters.

Up at the main house the sight of the huge timber supporting the loft reminded me of the summer day in 1973 when our first kids, complaining furiously but secretly proud of themselves, had lugged it across the island. Then I went on, past Bishop Loring's Chapel sign still hanging on the outhouse, to the barn. Chickens and guineas set up their usual commotion in the barnyard, and Arnold, now grown to enormous size, came lumbering up to get his ears scratched. Helga and Zelda, our matronly sows, followed behind him. On a more efficient farm those two would long since have been turned to sausage, but Sue Heywood had so lobbied for women's rights that we hadn't butchered them. I supposed now I would have to do it.

Tearing everything down was not going to be easy. I wondered if I could get permission to burn the buildings. Not a bad idea. Light it off and let it rip. Get the press in to watch. Shoot the pigs and throw Benny's half-finished go-cart onto the funeral pyre, while former students sang Tommy's song "I'm Just A Boy," to the accompaniment of the crackling flames. Not a bad idea at all! I bet a scene like that would generate enough maudlin media coverage to make those bastards in Boston really squirm.

I wallowed a while in satisfying thoughts of revenge before catching myself up short. What right had I to send up eight years' worth of a lot of people's work and dreams literally in smoke? Besides, what profit was there in siccing the media on the bureaucrats at DYS? They might squirm a bit, but even while they squirmed they would know that they had won. Cost wasn't the only reason we had been shut down. Penikese had in a small way rocked the boat. Our insistence on trying to really rehabilitate a few kids rather than just "cool off" a lot of them had raised some awkward issues, and the people we made uncomfortable wanted to get rid of us. They knew the media had short memories and that once closed Penikese would soon be forgotten.

I decided we weren't going to be shoved aside that easily. I wish I could say that I was motivated to carry on because of the kids. That had something to do with it—I still wanted to be that doctor— but mainly I was mad. Perhaps if the department's spokesmen had been candid enough to admit there were just too many delinquents in the system to permit the level of effort per individual that Penikese represented, I might have felt differently. Instead Assistant Commissioner Ned Loughran, whose competence made him DYS's point man when things got hot, had chosen to field our local newspaper's inquiries about us by saying Penikese was not being refunded because we were "underutilized and too expensive."

That had pissed me off. "Too expensive" suggested we had been wasting taxpayers' money or perhaps worse. "Underutilized" implied we weren't any good. I didn't mind being dismissed as a failed idealist, but I did mind being called incompetent and perhaps dishonest, even if only by inference. To allow Penikese to go under would let those charges stand. So one way or another we would have to prove Loughran wrong. Then perhaps I could move on to something else.

The Joseph Perini Foundation put up $10,000 to keep us going through the summer. David Masch, John McRoberts, and I stayed on the payroll to explore other options for the school, and the rest of the staff went full time on to their other jobs. Our target date for reopening was September 1981.

We had our old friend Harold "Red" Hill to thank for that $10,000, and without it we would not have survived. Red Hill had been a pioneer aviator until he married a girl who hated flying, so he made an unlikely career change to become an antiques appraiser. Others with a similar background might have found this kind of work too sedate, but Red made his own excitement whatever he did. He was probably the most completely happy man I ever met and certainly the only one who could mean it when he said, "If I had to do it all over again, I wouldn't change a thing." On his seventy-fifth birthday his wife lifted her ban against flying, and the two of them went off to Texas to a museum of still-functioning antique aircraft where Red checked out an ancient Steerman and put it through its paces. He never had much money of his own, but through his work he knew many people who did. I first met him in his capacity as chairman of a foundation that had been set up by his old fishing partner, Joseph Perini. Red had a soft spot for unlucky children and so called up one day to say that he had read about Penikese and wondered if we needed any money. This led to his visit to the island, after which he became almost part of the staff. For his role as honorary boat captain he bought an absurd yachting cap in which he took great pleasure.

The only time I ever saw Red really mad was when he learned that DYS was closing down "his" school. "Oh, the bastards!" he stormed and was all set to call his influential connections to the governor until I talked him out of it. I had already thought of mobi-

lizing friends of the school who might be able to put political
pressure on DYS, but I knew that even if we prevailed it would
be a Pyrrhic victory. By controlling what kids Penikese got sent,
the department held all the cards.

Red, however, would not be talked out of approaching his fellow
trustees at the Perini Foundation to get us an emergency grant to
keep the school alive until we came up with an alternative use for
it. The trustees were understandably unhappy at giving $10,000 to
a nonfunctioning organization, but Red prevailed. "Joe would have
wanted it," he told them, and no one could argue with the man
who had been Joe Perini's best friend.

The most promising of the new initiatives David, John and I considered was a joint program between Penikese and the Perkins
School for the Blind in Boston that would test the idea of using
the island for a combined enrollment of delinquents and handicapped adolescents. Our DYS kids talked tough but gave up easily. We thought it would be a good lesson for them to be around
kids who, despite real handicaps, had the courage to keep plugging.
We also thought they would profit from learning to help others.
What was in this arrangement for the Perkins kids was less clear,
but I knew they would have fun on the island, and I thought they
might gain something from learning to cope with an environment
that made fewer concessions to their handicaps than did Perkins.
We got a grant from the R. K. Mellon Foundation to underwrite
a pilot program which we ran in July and August on Penikese and
aboard the replica of Joshua Slocum's famous yawl *Spray* which two
former Penikese staff members, John Burman and Diana Stinson,
had built and were living aboard.

John and Diana ran this program with enormous skill and patience. Watching blind boys and girls learn, from touching the model
John built for them, how to move confidently around a pitching
deck was a fine thing. So was seeing our own tough guy, Mike,
unselfconsciously guiding his blind friends into the dingy. The only
dropout that summer was one of our former students, David, who
"freaked out" at the sight of physical handicaps and quit.

I was proud of this effort, which in many ways came closer than
anything else to my original plans for the school. But Perkins had

no interest in our proposal for a long-term affiliation involving more joint summer projects and the use of our Woods Hole dormitory as a halfway house to help blind kids make the transition from school to living on their own. So that was the end of that.

September came and went. The negotiations we had begun with the Massachusetts Department of Education to get the school accredited to accept special-needs students directly from local school systems were bogged down in a sea of red tape. We were getting increasingly desperate. In an effort to free ourselves entirely from public support we launched a quixotic effort to make Penikese self-supporting through the mail-order sale of island-grown food products and outdoor furniture. To test the feasibility of this scheme, John and I designed templates and jigs for mass-producing a functionally handsome piece of furniture we called the Penikese Island Porch Chair. We built the prototype, photographed it, and took out an ad in the December issue of *Yankee* magazine. *Yankee* reached an audience of 875,000 people then and claimed somewhere around a 3-percent response to their advertisements.

In anticipation of 26,250 orders we began making plans to bring back some of our own former students and some from Perkins to set up production. To supplement the $20 profit we expected on each chair, David conceived the idea of talking to funeral directors with the proposal that they approach their clients with the idea of bequests to Penikese "as a living memorial for their loved ones." This idea unfortunately failed to sell, and so did the chairs. Two out of those 875,000 readers sent in orders, leaving us with profits of $40 against a loss of the $1,200 we paid for the advertisement. December, as it turned out, is the worst month for mail-order sales, of whatever kind.

Self-sufficiency remained our objective, but selling outdoor furniture in midwinter was apparently not the right way to attain it. We put off reopening the school until the following spring. Garfield Arthur, one of our now out-of-work former staff, contracted to winter over on Penikese to look after our livestock and buildings. I joined him there after cold weather had set in late in November, and we went about the sad task of slaughtering Helga and Zelda. David took a temporary job directing another program. John set himself up as a paving contractor, and the rest of our staff drifted off to other pursuits. Franny Shepherd, who as our bookkeeper had for years quietly been holding the school together, volunteered to stay on in the office, and that winter I discovered she had right along been putting her own money into our depleted coffers.

On February 6, 1982, I convened a panel of Penikese Island Corporation members and other friends of the school in Woods Hole to decide if we had come to the end of the line. This group urged us to keep going and pitched in to help us do so. John McElligott of DYS undertook to get us set up with a rate structure that would allow us to accept referrals from any state agency rather than just DYS. The Mellon Foundation made us another grant that enabled us to hire Susie Devlin, an experienced special-needs teacher, to push through our accreditation by the Department of Education, and Peter Foliejeski of the Department of Mental Health began working with us to set up a program for DMH kids that included a residential summer program on Penikese and a day school in Woods Hole during the academic year.

Penikese reopened to students on July 6, 1982. Our funding came once again from a purchase-of-service contract, but we hoped that drawing students from the departments of Social Services (DSS) and Mental Health (DMH), along with DYS, would give us a broad enough base of referrals to keep enrollment above the break-even point. We lost money that summer, but at a sustainable rate thanks to the continuing support of friends, foundations and Franny.

When our day school opened in September we found ourselves stretched pretty thin trying to operate two programs with only six staff. So we reluctantly closed down on the island again at Christmas, and Garfield returned to his solitary duty as caretaker. January and February had always been both the riskiest and most expensive months to operate on Penikese. We planned to reopen in March of 1983.

The day school, with Anne Driscoll, David Clemence-Schreiner and me as instructors, was a new experience. DYS kids, for all their faults, were full of life. Some of our DMH kids, by contrast, were withdrawn to the point of being almost totally inert. We had our first suicide attempt that winter when a boy who found death preferable to doing arithmetic poured paint thinner in his coffee and drank it. What scared me most about that incident was that the boy involved had no conception of what dying was all about. The countless TV characters he had seen "blown away" had all revived in time for the next show, and I guess he figured the same thing would happen with him. His suicide attempt gave him a certain celebrity, so whenever he was upset or things were slow he would try again and then lie back to bask in all the ensuing attention. Evidently what had saved him the first time was the milk in his coffee.

We did have a couple of pretty lively girls in the program who kept things interesting. I taught a current events course that occasionally produced some remarkably adult discussions. One class that I was particularly proud of had as its topic the merits of the law which required birth-control clinics to notify the parents of minors to whom they had provided contraceptives. A very bright girl named Jennifer led the argument for the parents' right to know, while normally silent Kenny became spokesman for the group who felt the measure was self-defeating since kids wouldn't use the clinics if they knew their parents would hear about it. The debate became so heated that our class went into overtime. Oddly, when I asked them about the same subject a couple of weeks later, they had forgotten all about it. I'm not sure whether the ability to retain information is an acquired one that these kids had never learned or whether short memories are just another symptom of children who live entirely in the present.

David and Anne were more pragmatic in their expectations for our students than I. They concentrated on drumming in necessary "survival skills," while I lobbied for the proposition that we did our kids the same disservice as their previous schools had done by making too many concessions to their alleged inability to learn anything. I am still not entirely willing to concede this point, even though David and Ann did teach our illiterates enough to pass their drivers-license tests, while I produced no Shakespearian scholars.

The day school, unfortunately, brought the same problems to Woods Hole as had Job Training. Two of our students broke into a neighbor's house. The owner chose not to press charges, but the boys were thrown out, and the year ended on an unhappy note.

The island reopened as planned and held its own financially during the summer of 1983, but the strain on the staff was beginning to tell. Our decision to make the program coeducational had achieved its intended goal of increasing referrals but at a cost of introducing a whole range of new problems the staff had to deal with. "At last!" announced our veteran staff member, Tom "Gramps" Buckley, "we've found the solution to maintaining enrollment. We'll breed our own students." There was a growing feeling that we were just spinning our wheels. Kids came, stayed a while and left, rarely to be heard from again. Our DYS graduates had stayed in touch, even when they were writing us from jail. This new crew, coming mostly from DMH and DSS, were in a paradoxical way both more passive and harder to work with than delinquents. Faced with a choice between hyperactivity and bland indifference, we preferred hyperactivity. It seemed increasingly as if the sole purpose of our efforts was to keep the school alive. The faceless teenagers who came drifting through the place might just as well have been someplace else — anyplace else, for that matter. Nothing seemed to touch them. Morale hit an all-time low. Torn between loyalty and frustration, the staff kept on plugging, but there wasn't much excitement left in Penikese for any of us.

That, basically, was the situation I dumped on David.

21

I N OCTOBER OF 1983 I left with my family to spend six months in Brazil. Thanks to their Brazilian mother, my own two boys were citizens of two countries, and Yara wanted them at least to see what their choice was before they turned eighteen and had to decide whether to be Americans or Brazilians. We had been planning this trip for a long time and deferred it every time Penikese had a crisis. Finally, Yara would wait no longer. David replaced me as director. I left him with a sinking ship, and he managed to keep it afloat until I got back the following April. The day school, however, did not survive. After a shaky start in September with a group of kids even more unstable than those of the previous year, the program limped along until late winter, by which time all of the original students were in jails or asylums, and there were no new ones coming.

I had saddled David with one other unworkable arrangement before I left. In an effort to get the members of our corporation more actively involved and also to take some of the load off our staff, I tried to set up committees of members to oversee virtually every aspect of the school's operation. There were nine of these committees all told, with mandates ranging from Island Safety to Income-Producing Projects. Only one ever really got off the ground. The Finance Committee, whose work was carried on by Mary Louise Montgomery, DeWitt "Dick" Jones, Nathaniel Pulsifer, John McRoberts and my old boss from the Oceanographic, Paul Fye, began the school's first effort at long-range financial planning. Dick's and Nat's computer model, which showed the financial implications of various operational alternatives, indicated several possible options that on paper at least would generate sufficient operating income to cover expenses.

That prospect provided a beacon of hope. Shortly after my return from Brazil, David and I sat down to ponder our choices. Continuing to limp along as we had been was out of the question. Either we had to make one last big push to put Penikese back on its feet or else close down by choice rather than by necessity later on. It wasn't an easy decision. Time after time over the past eleven years we had flogged up renewed enthusiasm to get things rolling again only to have whatever momentum we were able to generate gradually fizzle out. On the other hand those eleven years would go for nothing if we let the school collapse. If the Finance Committee could alleviate our ongoing worry about how to pay the bills, it was probably worth another shot. We would share the job. David would become Dean of Students, and I would look after operations. Since our computer model only included $20,000 to pay one director, we split that amount between us. David got the other half of his salary as a relief staff member on the island, and I got my other half for running the boat.

Since then we have been, as the kids would say, "on a roll." Penikese's renaissance was due to a number of factors which all finally came together. The eight nonfunctioning committees of the corporation were disbanded, and the Finance Committee became our Executive Committee, which meets monthly. Five heads are better than one, particularly when that one is mine, and the Executive Committee, more than anything else, has been responsible for the school's improved financial health and the sense of optimism that follows from it. We began an endowment fund. Staff salaries, although still so low most of us continue to work at other jobs, have become at least competitive with what other alternative schools are able to pay. We finally got a really good boat. Nat Pulsifer led the fund-raising drive that raised the $100,000 we put into a rugged thirty-six-foot hull that is dry, able and quiet—in short everything that our previous boats were not. The *Harold M. Hill*, named after Red, who died in 1985, has taken away a lot of my anxiety whenever the phone rings on dark and stormy nights. Nat went so far over his target that we had money enough left for a new pier as well, and that makes my job even easier.

Everyone else's morale has also improved. Gone was the uncertain feeling that comes from being part of an organization constantly on the brink of calamity. Our two veteran staffers, Tom White and Susie Devlin, now with nearly sixteen years of experience between them, set the tone for a staff that maintains as high standards as we've ever had. Our instructors still work alternate full-week shifts, but tension is so much reduced on the island that this schedule is less backbreaking than before.

Tension is less because the students we are getting are better suited to being on Penikese. Most of our kids again come from DYS, thanks to David, who reestablished relations with the DYS people I offended with my constant criticism. The department itself is also improved. A coherent philosophy has finally evolved from the shambles left years earlier by Jerome Miller. Accountability is now emphasized, to the point that caseworkers require their kids to sign Contracts of Conditional Liberty which stipulate what they must do to earn their discharge and what the consequences will be if they don't do it. Caseworkers themselves seem older, more realistic and more professional than the ones we worked with from 1973 to 1981. What problems remain are more the fault of the law-and-order zealots than of DYS. Mandatory confinement for violent crimes, which was a concession made to Governor King's Task Force on Juvenile Crime, proved to be a poor policy. The two murderers we have had on the island were basically gentle kids who were driven to violence by terror. Both were far better prospects for rehabilitation than many habitual offenders whose numerous crimes were all against property. Today those two boys would have to be locked up for a year in the company of some pretty sick customers. No good can come of that.

We owe our new-found stability also to the fact that Penikese has grown respectable in its old age. The school finally got a license from the Office for Children thanks to the Cuttyhunk selectmen, who in their triple capacities as health, fire and safety inspectors for the Town of Gosnold broke through a ten-year-old logjam by declaring the school safe and healthy, thus freeing OFC from having to make that determination on its own. Even more remarkable, the Department of Education accredited Penikese's educational program in 1986. Susie Devlin worked long hours to achieve this triumph, but she never would have pulled it off had she not found a powerful ally from the Department of Education in the person of Dick Frigault. Dick is one of those rare public officials who look at content instead of form. He spent enough time on Penikese to see that a lot of teaching is being done in ways too unconventional to conform to his department's regulations and he had the courage to go way out on a limb to get the school accredited.

All this could change. Penikese will always be a fragile organization. We were almost put out of business in 1985 when for a month we were unable to renew our public-liability-insurance policy. One bad accident could close the school. Changing political winds also affect us. Our luck in attracting qualified staff may not hold if the Yuppies prevail. Massachusetts could find some other use for the island. (Some nut discovered that the law empowering Massachusetts to exile lepers to Penikese was still on the books and recently proposed using Penikese as a place to banish "promiscuous" AIDS carriers.)

Whatever happens, everyone who has worked on Penikese has the satisfaction of knowing he or she did a hard job as well or better than it has ever been done before. The things we accomplished are on record. In June 1986 the National Geographic Society commissioned an Academy Award-winning film maker, Nigel Noble, to make a documentary about the school. His film could not show all the staff and all the kids who have been at Penikese since 1973, but one scene does capture in a remarkable way the spirit of the school we all built. That scene, shot against the setting sun, shows all the boys and staff together raising the huge timber wall of our new post-and-beam school house. Everyone puts his shoulder into the job, backs strain and the wall slowly rises. It almost stops. The crew makes one last enormous effort, and it clunks massively into place. That wall looks solid enough to last a long time.

EPILOGUE

BILLY IS LEAVING to go to high school. He had come to Penikese on the same day that Nigel Noble's film crew began shooting, and the opening scene of the National Geographic film shows
him arriving. "An island," says Billy. "I like that."

He liked Penikese, and we liked him. Now, seven months later,
he will be the last of our movie stars to graduate, and we are going
to miss him. His stay here has been productive. He and Susie Devlin
have worked hard to get him accepted into his hometown vocational school. If I remember correctly, the last time Billy went to
school on a regular basis was as a fifth grader.

Normally he would finish up with us on Friday when the rest
of the gang come in for their weekends at home, but he has a
meeting to go to at his new school, so I am going down to bring
him in on this cold, clear January Wednesday afternoon.

Everybody is on the pier when I come alongside. Lunch was
evidently a going-away party. Billy, standing there next to his bag,
looks a little lost in the middle of all the hollering and backslap-
ping. He jumps aboard and somebody yells "Faggot!" The rest of
the gang picks up the chant. *"Faa-gut! Faa-gut! Faa-gut!"*

Billy grins. This is an old joke dating back to a time when he
punched a boy who called him queer. Tom White, who broke up
the fight, decreed that everyone would start calling Billy "Faggot"
to desensitize him to this unfounded accusation. The nickname
stuck, and now Faggot is going home.

"You want to drive?" I ask him.

"Sure."

"OK, you see Can Number Three over there? Head to pass that one on your left."

"Hey! It ain't like I never done this before, right?"

"Right." Still, I stand behind him as he rounds Number 3 and heads for Number 5.

"You want me to set the loran for Lone Rock?" Billy asks. "It's waypoint number five, ain't it?"

"Yeah, go ahead. Jesus, Billy! You're getting pretty good. You don't need me any more, that's for sure."

I sit down and make a point not to look out the window. Billy is proud of himself, and I won't spoil it by looking over his shoulder. He twiddles with the loran. "Fifteen knots, not bad," he says more to himself than to me. I have nothing to worry about with this kid.

As usual the diesel's mesmerizing drone soon has me daydreaming. I recall that wild night when Stan ran the old *Nereis* across to Cuttyhunk. Last I heard Stan was in New Mexico and doing alright. Of the same bunch from 1973, Duane has dropped from sight, Danny is a male prostitute, and Nick and Bill are locked up. Little Jack did a stretch for manslaughter, but he is out now. From what I understand, he beat up the neighborhood child molester. The man died.

How long ago was all that? Good Lord, I've been at this game almost fourteen years! Funny, I still think of myself as a Marine, but I've got more time in now with Penikese than I had on active duty. I guess that makes me a social worker. Not quite the kind of career I first had in mind.

Let's see, 13 years, 6 months, take away the time I was in Brazil gives me 676 weeks times, say, an average of 3 trips a week which works out to 2,028 round trips to Penikese Island. Probably a world record.

Two thousand and twenty-eight boat trips, give or take a couple of hundred either way. Scared kids going down. Happy kids coming back. Good trips and bad trips. The worst ones had had nothing to do with the weather. Was it Tom White who said his heart skipped a beat whenever he saw me pull in to the pier unexpectedly? He had good reason. Too often the boat has been the messenger of misfortune. Four staff have lost close family members in the span of our school's short history. One who died was David's son.

That was the most tragic irony of all. Matthew Masch, son of the man who has been Pops to so many boys, drowned in 1979. I think I would crack if one of my boys drowned, but David kept going. His world record is more impressive than mine. He has spent longer living with difficult kids on Penikese Island than any man alive. No mean feat.

"The Evil Island" is what one historian called Penikese, and it does seem as if those fated to live on the island have had more than their share of misfortune. But that historian is wrong. Penikese has been responsible for more good than bad. Billy is the island's latest beneficiary, and he will not be its last.

Our newest graduate is playing with the loran again.

"Hey, George! We're comin' up on Lone Rock. What's the next waypoint?"

"Nine. That's the one that takes you between Weepecket and Naushon, but you don't need it, do you? You can see a hundred miles on a day like this."

"Yeah, I can see alright, but I like fuckin' with the loran.

"OK, have at it, but remember, that loran doesn't have eyes. You've got to look where you're going."

"Want me to turn on the radar?"

"No! I want you to look out the window."

"Radar's more fun. It's all we got, seein' as you won't let us have no TV."

"Shut up and keep your eyes on the road!"

Radar and loran were both too expensive for us even to think about in 1973. A lot has changed in fourteen years. A lot has not. Some things that seemed obvious to me in the beginning seem less obvious now. David has always been more realistic about this business than I have. So has John McElligott. I am only now beginning to realize what they knew all along. There can be no breakthroughs. There is no button we can push to make delinquency go away. Short of overhauling our whole society, what we are already doing is about all that we can hope to do.

When we began I assumed delinquents were responding logically to the world they lived in. I gave our kids credit for making logical choices based on limited options, and I thought if I could expand their options to include the right choices they would make the right choices.

That's why I was so hooked on the idea of accountability. I thought we could turn delinquents around by rewarding good behavior and punishing bad. I had so little patience with people who objected to punishment for high-minded reasons because I felt that not holding delinquents accountable made already confused boys even more confused. I believed that children wanted limits. Take a baby out of the security of his crib, and he gets scared. Turn a delinquent loose with no clearer guideline to behavior than "feeling good about himself," and he gets scared too. Accountability provides limits. It gives a kid the security of knowing what is going to happen, or so I thought.

Jonesy should have taught me that delinquents don't necessarily make the connections that seemed so obvious to me. Jonesy didn't know how to make connections at all. The only thing real for him was now. If you wanted an acolyte for your altar guild, Jonesy would be your man. If you wanted a guard for your concentration camp, he'd do fine at that also. There was no Jonesy. He was whatever his surroundings made him into.

How did he get that way? If I had to pick a single influence that made Jonesy the way he was, I would point to his parents — or more properly, to the world his parents created for him. Not even those Chinese interrogators could have conceived of a more random, nightmarish world than the one Mr. Jones' mercurial brutality and Mrs. Jones' double-speak produced for their son. In a senseless universe, anything goes. Coming from a childhood that offered zero predictability, Jonesy became a chameleon that adjusted, with seeming effortlessness, to the dominant influence of the moment.

My idea of teaching accountability by using a self-contained little island where everything makes sense had not worked for boys like Jonesy whose random childhoods had left them incapable of connecting cause and effect. "Scared Straight," that briefly publicized program that showed young delinquents the horrors of prison, had not worked for the same reason. The assumption there was that a boy who met a lifer would come away thinking, "If I do what he did, I'll end up where he is." But someone who has been raised

as Jonesy was raised cannot think that way. We were as unsuccessful
in showing Jonesy that too much sugar made him morose as we
were in trying to scare him straight with ten days of jail. The evidence of what alcohol had done to his father did not stop him from
getting drunk himself. He just couldn't add it all up. Jonesy was
such a good con artist because he believed his own line. He saw
himself as the victim of influences he could not control, and the
sad thing is that he was probably right. Maybe a terrified little boy
who hides, as Jonesy did, under his bed while his drunken father
beats his mother learns to tune out forever the part of his brain
that deals with reality. Maybe what we call a criminal mind is one
that has developed the best defense against a world that makes no
sense. The certainty is that once an individual reaches the point
where he can no longer make connections he becomes a very scary
person. He is also beyond our help, because we have no way to
reach him. Our world is not his world.

Billy is eyeing me furtively. He sees I am watching him and pulls
a cigarette out of his pocket with a great flourish. Then he pretends
he is going to light it.

"No way, you turkey! Not even graduates get to smoke those goddamn things on this boat."

He laughs. Billy knows how much I hate cigarettes. That's another
one of my failed crusades. I would like to have banned smoking
at the school, but was advised against it. Apparently nicotine dependence increases with stress, and kicking the habit creates more
stress, so you have a vicious circle. Our kids are under enough stress
already. Also, half the staff smokes, so I have limited my crusade
to bribery. Anybody who quits for three months gets $50. So far
there have been no takers.

"You been sleepin'?" asks Billy.

"No, just thinking."

"Yeah? What about?"

"About a kid a lot like you who was here a long time ago. He
was also good around boats, but he didn't make it. You are going
to make it, right?"

"Right! I'm done doin' crime."

"How come?"

"Dunno, I like doin' this kind o' stuff better. You know, drivin' boats an' shit like that. Tom tell you he's givin' me a job next summer?"

"I heard. You must be doing something right, Billy. You're only the second kid in eight years that Tom's hired."

Tom White runs a construction business when he's not running his shift on the island. I think he'll get his money's worth out of Billy.

I have been sneaking furtive looks out the window, but I don't let on. "Where are we, Captain?"

"Just comin' up to them Weepeckers or whatever you call 'em."

"Weepeckets is what we call them. Watch out for that line of rocks that runs off to the south of the big island."

"Don't worry. No way I'm gonna hit a rock today. I'm goin' home."

"Good. Then I can go back to sleep. Holler when you get to Number Thirteen."

I go back to my thinking. What do you do when nothing works? That's the question I am left with after fourteen years of looking for an answer. What else can we do except more of the same? David once made the analogy between our work and the triage system army field hospitals use when they are overwhelmed with too many wounded. The triage system dictates that both the critically wounded and the soldiers sure to survive are ignored so that the hospital's limited staff can concentrate its efforts on the group whose survival depends on help. Too bad we can't do the same thing. If right from the start we could sort kids by our statistician Woolcott Smith's Success Index, then Penikese, at least, could refuse to accept "poor prospects" and devote its efforts to turning "fair prospects" into "good" ones. By concentrating on the kids who could swing either way, our success rate would be at least 50 percent.

The trouble is, we can't do that. Jonesy carried the seeds of his own destruction with him on the day he first set foot on Penikese, but there was no way we could have known it. He was a survivor. The same nightmare world that would have driven a weaker kid into withdrawal or suicide had taught him that chameleonlike ability to adapt instinctively to whatever an unpredictable fate threw at him. That's why the most badly damaged kids are the ones who most easily fool us. They fit in easily, speak plausibly and seem like they have it all together. Boys with more visible problems may be better prospects. They may not. We don't know, because there are no patterns. So we have to give every kid a chance.

The attitudes I attributed to muddleheadedness among the reformers are probably based on a better appreciation than I had for how unpredictable this business really is. It is all the harder to write a boy off as beyond hope when the chance is so good of being wrong. Still I think we can no more avoid making this choice than the surgeon faced with too many wounded men can avoid writing off the critically injured. My system for rehabilitation based on accountability may not provide the universal cure I once predicted, but at least it relieves us from having to make subjective judgments in applying the triage system to delinquents. Letting the boy himself tell us by his own behavior whether or not he is salvageable may seem hard-hearted, but I can think of no other way to maximize the number we can save while protecting society from the ones we cannot.

I know now that at best our success rate will never be very high. Society's "safety net" provides so many filters a boy must pass through before he even gets to DYS that all but our most disturbed adolescents are segregated out of the group that finally arrives on Penikese. All things considered, I expect the 16-percent success figure our follow-up study came up with is representative of what the system overall can hope to accomplish. No system that selects out all but its most difficult cases can then expect to salvage everyone who is left.

So the question for me becomes whether even what we're doing now is worth the cost. Should taxpayers be paying us $92 per day to keep a boy on Penikese when eighty-four out of every hundred students sent us go home unrehabilitated? I think what on the face of it appears to be a pretty marginal return on the taxpayer's investment may not be such a bad investment after all. Sixteen percent is less discouraging a figure when considered against what those relatively few successes would otherwise have cost society in dollars and misery if the investment were not made. Sixteen percent also does not give a complete picture of the results. If Penikese can make even the most disturbed boy marginally better, that is progress, even if it will never show up statistically.

Certainly no hospital would make less of an effort on behalf of a patient whose disease gives him only a 16-percent chance of recovery. Neither should we, because delinquency is a disease every bit as horrible as any of the physical afflictions society is so much more willing to combat. Can you see Jerry Lewis raising millions to help delinquents? Not likely. We find in every kid who comes to Penikese the ruins of the boy he might have been if the combination of heredity, poor nutrition and environment had not so crippled him. Can there be any worse disease for a child than to be turned into a monster nobody can love? Delinquents, like addicts and AIDS victims, elicit fear and contempt rather than sympathy. So perhaps I have ended up becoming a doctor of sorts after all. A doctor who saves only sixteen out of every hundred of his patients cannot claim to be a very good one, but at least he does have the satisfaction of knowing all his patients are a bit better off than they would have been without him.

"How we doing on fuel, Billy?"

"Port tank's on a quarter, starboard one's about empty. We're usin' the port side, so we're OK. But you're gonna need more before you go back out."

"OK, remind me to call the truck when we get in." David and I may be running out of fuel, too, pretty soon. Odd, how the idea of leaving Penikese was harder to face during the years when I was less sure of the school's value and more desperate just to keep the place afloat. Now finally all the leaks have been pretty well plugged up. Politicians or insurance men could still sink us, but barring that, Penikese will survive. Huge outpourings of energy from many people have at last infused the school with a life of its own. I expect that fourteen years from now, our successors will still be wrestling with all the same problems, and I know that by then another four hundred or so kids will at the very least have found on Penikese that one good experience which John McElligott once reminded me they would not otherwise have had.

I look at Billy, and I see that my years here have been well spent. I also see that he is weaving all over the ocean. "Billy! What's going on?"

"Lobster pots! I'm tryin' not to hit 'em. Jesus! They're all over the place in here."

"Well, don't hit any of the red-and-gold ones. Those are mine."

"Red and gold? I already run over a couple of those!"

"You do, my friend, and that fifty bucks Franny's giving you for graduating is going right into my pocket."

"Yeah? First you're gonna have to catch me! You want me to go right up to Number Thirteen or can I cut it?"

We are coming into Woods Hole. I stand up. "Go ahead and cut it. Just watch your depth. There's shoal water off Timmy's Point there."

Billy heads for Red Number 10.

"What's the buoy rule?" I ask him.

"Red Right Returnin'."

"Are we leaving or returning when we go through Woods Hole heading east?"

"Leavin', so I keep the red ones on my left. Hey, I know this stuff! You don't have to keep askin' me."

"Yes, you've learned a lot. You remember when you first came down here? You wouldn't even take your turn at the wheel your first couple of trips."

"Yeah, I remember, but I was different then. I was scared. I ain't scared now."

Billy makes the landing, and we walk up to Penikese House to find Franny. On the way, I stop at the Post Office to get the mail. There is a letter from Tom Buckley, who has retired from Penikese to become a dealer in antique books and letters. He has sent me an ancient postcard from his collection. On the front in bold block letters is printed a good Victorian truism. It says: ANY BOY WORTH SAVING WILL SAVE HIMSELF.

CASTAWAYS: THE PENIKESE ISLAND EXPERIMENT
WAS DESIGNED BY HANS TEENSMA AND MICHAEL GRINLEY OF IMPRESS
AND TYPESET IN ELANTE, A FILM VERSION OF ELECTRA.